Learning and the Marketplace

Alison Kirk

Learning
AND THE
Marketplace

A PHILOSOPHICAL,
CROSS-CULTURAL
(and Occasionally Irreverent)

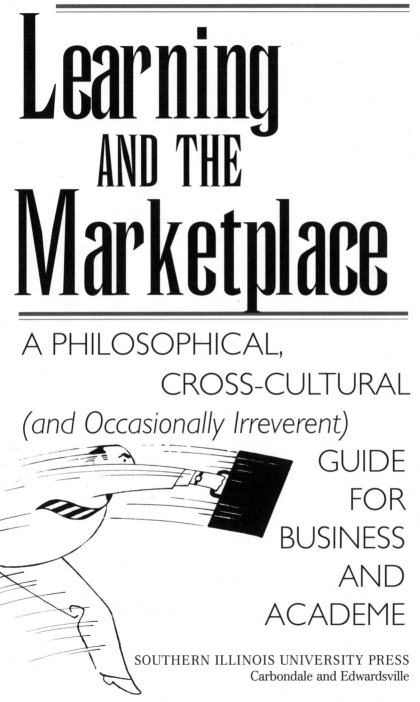

GUIDE
FOR
BUSINESS
AND
ACADEME

SOUTHERN ILLINOIS UNIVERSITY PRESS
Carbondale and Edwardsville

Library of Congress Cataloging-in-Publication Data

Kirk, Alison, 1945–
    Learning and the marketplace : a philosophical, cross-cultural (and
occasionally irreverent) guide for business and academe / Alison Kirk.
        p.   cm.
    1. Industrial management—Terminology.   2. School management and
organization—Terminology.   3. Business—Terminology.   4. Education—
Terminology.   I. Title.
HD30.17.K57   1996
650—dc20   96-13122
                                                                                        CIP
ISBN 0-8093-2092-4 (alk. paper)
ISBN 0-8093-2068-1 (pbk. : alk. paper)

*Caricatures are by Lawrence Lazarus,
copyright © 1996 by Lawrence Lazarus.*

For my mother and father,
with love and gratitude

Contents

Contents

Master, Mastery; Measurement; Mentor (and Advisor);
Merit Pay; Metaphor; Mission; Money; Moral Education,
Morality, Moral Reasoning; Motivation; The Carrot
and the Stick

xi

X, Y, Z: Yin, Yang, and NA   176

Theories X and Y; Is Mutual Learning Possible?;
Theory Z; Zero Defects; Zero Sum; Zip

Appendixes

Contents

Preface

As a book more intent on asking than on answering questions, *Learning and the Marketplace* assumes there is no one way to learn, and its material is presented from a variety of perspectives. Readers are invited to use the book in the way that works best for them at the time they are picking it up. After all, a book is still a wonderfully flexible and interactive medium.

Some readers, of course, will want to use this volume as a dictionary that provokes thought. To zero in on specific entries, they'll find that our most ancient searching aid, the alphabetical arrangement, still works as originally designed.

Since most people, however, are used to reading straight through from beginning to end, *Learning and the Marketplace* is paced to be read as a continuous text. Themes and issues build chapter by chapter, and there are clear linkages within each chapter. Indeed, one of the accidental discoveries in the process of putting this book together was that our language, by some mysterious, associative principle, seems to cluster topics in certain parts of the alphabet.

Readers who can't tolerate an exclusive diet of abstract definition are offered the balance of illustrations, first-person commentaries, and personal-experience essays. The inspiration and authority for this mix, by the way, spring from my own childhood recollection of *Compton's Pic-*

tured Encyclopedia, which had essays and pieces of short fiction, often it seemed, about anthropomorphic animals, appearing as unexpected side trips among the learned, more factual entries.

Margins are meant to be written in. This is a book to talk back to, to correct, and to supplement. It doesn't claim that there is one right answer on everything, and it certainly shares Emerson's distrust of consistency for its own sake. As befits a learning document, *Learning and the Marketplace* provides discussion questions or references to other sections containing pertinent questions. It also provides a few projects for gathering more perspectives. Many readers, to be sure, will see other dilemmas to consider and discuss.

Basic questions on such topics as diversity, performance appraisal, fragmentation and integration, and the relationship between learning, working, and living are revisited regularly in the book, just as they are in life. In reading, as in firsthand experience, we usually don't grasp everything the first time; we need incremental repetition to gain depth. *Learning and the Marketplace* accepts that as a fact of life. Those who want to track themes or organize discussion groups should find the interlocking questions and the topical guides in the appendixes helpful tools. The recurring illustrations of the two men who caricature the business and academic mentalities, wherever they exist, also emphasize connections.

Overall, *Learning and the Marketplace* is designed with different learners in mind—linear and associative, abstract and concrete, left-brained and right. It assumes that we see what we're looking for and are ready to find, that we learn in the way that meets our needs and accords with our temperaments. Ideally, we also always find something more than we thought we would. Such, at least, is the hope behind the book.

Acknowledgments

The people I'd most like to thank do not necessarily approve of, or endorse, my every word or decision. Some would be surprised to find themselves thanked at all. A lesser conclusion from the experience of producing this book is that people often help without knowing that they have, or even meaning to. A far greater one is that the world abounds in extraordinarily generous people willing to give solely from a desire to be helpful.

I am, then, deeply grateful to the following for the roles they played in the unfolding of this book: Nancy Means Wright, my literary mentor and inspiration; Joseph R. Curry, Alexander A. Uhle, Stephen D. Bruce, and Ronald C. Pilenzo, providers of my basic learning experiences and continued stimulation; Harold Webber Jr., ever my technological Prometheus; Jeff Olson, K. K. Wilder, and Wendy Webber Nicholson, who provided sound and thoughtful advice on creating the book proposal; Lawrence Lazarus, artist, illustrator of this book, and most esteemed conversational philosopher; Dennis J. Hannan, James R. Barker, and Alice Z. Berninghausen, who served as readers of an early manuscript and provided generously detailed suggestions, corrections, and questions from the perspectives of educator, business executive, and involved parent, respectively; Carole Fenn, Dieuwke Davydov, Diana Fanning, my sources of ongoing personal support; James D. Simmons and Carol A. Burns at Southern Illinois University Press and copyeditor Rebecca Spears Schwartz, for their valuable professional expertise, sublime patience, sensitivity, and good cheer above and beyond the call of job descriptions; and finally, Walter G. Koenig, my true life partner and spouse, whose contributions have included personal counsel and support, technological assistance, an extensive knowledge of organizational psychology, an understanding of the physical universe, years of experience in multiple real worlds, including the classroom, and, above all, loyalty, comfort, and love. For their unwavering faith in me, I've dedicated this book to my parents.

Acknowledgments

Learning and the Marketplace

ABCs for Business and Academe

In schools and colleges, *academic* is a term of distinction, meaning serious, pure, intellectual, disciplined, intense. In business, if the word comes up at all (and that is unlikely), it means moot, not worth considering, theoretical, not applicable.

"It's academic" in the corporate world means it's irrelevant; forget it.

Business, on the other hand, always means something serious, something real. Making money is no laughing matter. When teachers tell their students to get down to business, they basically mean "wake up and smell the coffee."

In the business world, to say "I think we can do business" means "I think we speak the same language and share the same ground rules and assumptions."

It's not easy for business and education to do business. At question is how much they should.

I didn't always think business and academe needed a cross-cultural guide. In fact, when I first encountered the business mentality in a school, I was merely horrified. I wondered how American business, having failed in so many cases to place or even show in the global competition, could possibly expect to come in and rescue our educational system. It seemed *they* (businesspeople) could learn more from *us* (school people). Surely the best place for the old-style, top-down, theory-X business leaders to learn the "**Y**s" and wherefores of it all was in the democracy of learning. And only a little later, when people started urging more business involvement in education, I was amazed that the idea was even taken seriously.

But that was in the late 1970s, early 1980s. Since then, of course, there have been the landmark studies, the decade of school reform, some 140,000 corporate partnerships in education, privatization, vouchers, and the invention of schools for profit. Also since then, I have personally migrated from teaching and administering at the high school and college levels into business journalism, where I have found the new cast of characters, as Samuel Johnson found the human race, both better and worse than I'd expected. The best learners, it seems, do better at everything, including business.

My view, then, has changed, yet not so much that I've forgotten the old one. In fact, whenever I write or edit business books and articles, I get simultaneous flashes of what the same expressions would mean, or how they would be received, in the world of education. It's as though I can put on those old cardboard eyeglasses for viewing 3-D movies in the 1950s. Combining the business lens and the education lens turns a flat image into a round one, and the resulting picture is both vivid and sharp. Sometimes, it's even funny.

Other times, of course, it's not so funny. One clear conclusion from examining side by side the languages of business and education is that if people really want to run a school, college, or university "like a business," we have a serious semantic problem. It starts with the illusion that, as fellow Americans, we have a common language. Not so—and the simpler and more commonplace the words, the more dangerous the illusion.

Specialized jargon, to be sure, is always an obstacle to conversation, but at least everyone recognizes it for what it is and stops when necessary to ask for translation. But what about the times when the same familiar words have completely different connotations for the users? What about the times when the same phenomena go by completely different names? These are the very situations that occur constantly when educators are told to "mean business." Maybe they mean something else.

Invariably, during any fierce and protracted argument, there is a point when some would-be peacemaker says, "I think the argument here is merely semantic," as though confusion generated by language is not of *real* significance. Our words, however, construct and reflect our worlds, our perceptions, and our whole way of thinking. Differences of language often mirror differences in worldviews and values. We need to look carefully at the languages of business and education. In doing so, we also look into the beliefs of two major American institutions responding to late-twentieth-century change in characteristically different ways.

Our habitual illusion that we have a common language masks essential differences in culture that we depend on to keep our national equilibrium. It also masks the unexpected resemblances that make mutual learning possible. Unmasking this illusion makes it easier both to give credit where it's due and to agree to disagree when that's in order. We cannot think intelligently about how best to prepare the next generation for productive lives without defining both the relationship between business and education and its proper limits. And the medium for this thinking must, as ever, be language.

Of course, onlookers often laugh as a result of an unmasking. Laughter, after all, is an inevitable response to seeing sudden nakedness. It's also a great aid to learning, as any teacher or corporate trainer can attest.

A is for Appraisal

Absenteeism

The problem of people not showing up to work is common to business and education. They've also shared a common range of responses. On the soft end of the response spectrum are such strategies as helping workers/students; involving them; making things more interesting. On the hard end are techniques like docking pay, benefits, or privileges; giving bad grades or performance reviews; warning, suspending, (documenting), and dismissing.

In schools, the suspension/dismissal options sometimes raise an interesting philosophical question: is forced absence a suitable or effective punishment for voluntary absence? Teachers also often object to forced attendance (e.g., mandatory study hall) as a punishment. The problem is in treating as punishment something educators habitually present as a valuable, even pleasurable activity in itself (quiet study in a confined space).

The business environment lends itself far better to the exploitation of self-interest as motivator. The focus of schools is obscured by some remnant of altruism. Whereas business can point to the harm absenteeism does in visible and concrete forms (hurts productivity and profitability, burdens coworkers, can hurt your paycheck and job security), the damage caused by school absence is remote and seemingly self-contained.

Educators enamored of outdated metaphors have been thankful for decades that *school* rhymes with *mule*. Metamorphosis is a good poetic punishment for absenteeism.

Abstract

Developing the ability to think abstractly is the major learning task of adolescence. It is the key to transferable learning. A large proportion of adults never attain this ability and, for that reason, cannot understand definitions of the word *abstract*.

In business, *abstract* as a noun, with the accent on the first syllable, means a summary. Otherwise, as an adjective, it bears the common American meaning of "not real."

Businesspeople use abstract thinking a great deal when they are making mathematical projections about profits, market shares, returns on investment, and so on. Abstractions always seem much more manageable than concrete individuals.

Academic

In schools and colleges, *academic* is a term of distinction, meaning serious, intellectual, pure, disciplined, focused, intense. In business, if the word comes up at all (and that is unlikely), it means moot, not worth considering, theoretical, not applicable. "It's academic" in the corporate world means it's irrelevant; forget it.

Accountability (and Responsibility)

References to accountability have increased in both business and the schools, though business is more comfortable with a word that sounds mathematical. *Accountability* means taking the count. It conjures up agreeable images of bottom lines and score boards. People who see themselves primarily as people persons, whether in business or education, generally don't like quantitative measurements. (See Measurement.)

Before accountability came into such favor, educators used the word *responsibility*. Being responsible means being responsive—listening, reacting, interacting, adjusting. It implies going beyond the standards originally spelled out, using one's personal judgment. Its reference point lies in the broad realm of morality. The reference point for accountability is strictly external. According to *Webster's Ninth New Collegiate Dictionary*, it has a legalistic outlook, implying a threat of punishment for failure to measure up. Note that terrorists claim responsibility or credit for their bombings to underscore their moral justification. They don't claim accountability. They know they broke the law; the point is, they meant to.

Falling short by accountability standards lends itself to shame or disgrace; failure to exercise responsibility is cause for guilt. The schools' move toward accountability is a move toward strictness. When business discusses corporate responsibility, it is turning lofty.

Administration

Administration, usually "the Administration," is the educational equivalent of "Management" in business.

The original service orientation of education remains vestigially in this term based on *minister*, to serve. (A minister is, of course, a servant.) As educational administrators become more grandiose, they often start to refer to themselves as management.

Affect, Affective

The words *affect* and *affective* for educators pertain to feelings or the emotions. Most believe the so-called affective domain should be considered in educational planning along with the so-called cognitive domain; educators are concerned with the emotional as well as the intellectual growth of the student.

In business, *affective* and *affect* are misspellings for *effective* and *effect.*

Aggressive

Business considers *aggressive* a laudable word for seizing initiative and refusing ever to yield. Educators derive the word from *aggression* and consider it socially aberrant.

Anxiety

Anxiety is a generalized and brooding form of fear that derives much of its pain and intensity from its very vagueness. It's a particularly virulent strain of worrying about the unknown and the uncontrollable. Responsible persons are more likely to suffer anxiety than those who are merely accountable.

Inasmuch as the unknown and the uncontrollable are the very materials, subjects, and objects of instruction, schools are natural breeding grounds for anxiety. Educators try to disarm it in part by giving it a clinical sounding specificity—school anxiety, math anxiety, writing anxiety. (These conditions are also sometimes named for their results: school avoidance, math avoidance, writing avoidance.)

Business is far more successful at avoiding anxiety. Sustained by its can-do orientation, it doesn't acknowledge the condition with a word. The same phenomenon there has the architectural or engineering term of *stress*, which is a no-fault response to something physical and therefore real.

✦ ✦ ✦

Anxiety Avoidance
(or How a Future English Teacher
Dropped Out of Reading)

No one who knew me as a child would ever have predicted I'd spend so much of my life in and around schools. I dreaded, even hated, school as a youngster. To this day, whenever I see little kids walking along with their books, I feel sorry for them, as they march off to have their spirits bruised.

Attending an elementary school that didn't give grades didn't help. In first grade, the class was divided into three reading groups. I was in the Blue Group, which was the fast group. The Yellow Group was slightly larger. That was the average group. Barry Lindberger, the big, class bully who jumped on people's backs, Stephen Black, who enjoyed stomping on dog droppings in his snap-up galoshes, and one low-profile colorless individual whose name I can't remember were in the Red Group. They were the public-disgrace group.

We didn't have grades or official labels, but we did have invidious comparisons and humiliation. Occasionally, the teacher would say, "Today the Yellow Group read better than the Blue Group." It was clear from her tone that that was a scandalous violation of the natural order of things; there was never any question about what was ordained to be good, better, best.

Not knowing how to enhance our group performance, as a lone individual, I resorted to prayer. "Please, God," I'd pray over and over again when I was supposed to be sleeping, "let the Blue Group read well tomorrow." Invariably, after a night of such ardent prayer, I would wake up sick the next day and get to stay home.

By third grade, I couldn't take the pressure any more. At this point, the fast group had shrunk to four, and we were entirely unsupervised during reading period. I wanted to read, but the other three wanted to have races to see who could finish the story first. Janet Barnard, Vivian Banish, and Johnny Fleming would all whip through the pages as fast as their stubby little fingers could flip them, laughing and arguing over who'd finished first.

I went to the teacher and said I couldn't keep up with my group and wanted to move down. She looked surprised, and my ex-teammates looked stunned. I didn't know it was bad form to avoid competition or request a demotion.

To the best of my recollection, I never connected with any reading group after that, but I did get a reward. In my self-instructing mode, I kept getting stuck on the word *determined.* This was because I was pronouncing it "*dete*rmined." "Debtor-mind," it sounded like. Sort of made sense, but not in context.

Who knows what made it fall into place for me, but suddenly, there it was, bursting out of my mouth. "Ah, de*ter*mined!!"

As with so much else in life, it was just a matter of finding the right place to put the stress.

✦ ✦ ✦

Appraisal

Appraisal, as in performance appraisal, is widely used in business. The word among educators for judging performance is *evaluation.* (See Evaluation.)

According to Webster, *appraise* usually implies "the fixing by an expert of the monetary worth of a thing," while *evaluate* implies the effort to determine the worth of something "in terms other than monetary."

Business rushes to embrace quantitative, monetary measurement. Schools stand back and judge value and quality, both of which—curiously—have become very hot business terms.

This might be a place to note, too, that schools rarely fire students or teachers while the school year is in progress. Consequences of poor performance are delayed and generally conveyed indirectly over an excruci-

atingly protracted period of time. (See Employment at Will.) Increasingly, business suffers the same problems as fears of litigation over wrongful discharge grow.

Sometimes it's hard to distinguish the model from the imitator, as in the relationship between life and art.

Aptitude (and Potential)

Here is a word primarily from the educational arena. School authorities must assess two things: what the student *can* do and what the student *does* do. *Could* and *would* are both important in education. Business can just focus on *did* or *didn't.*

The closest equivalent in business to education's aptitude is called "potential." Sometimes it's determined by testing but more often by the instinct of the appraiser. Appraisers better not make too many bad judgment calls, of course. Business, after all, focuses on performance.

Athlete

Admiration for the athlete is one of our few genuine cultural touchstones. Sports are universally hailed as the great training ground for life, by which most Americans mean the business world. In our athletic models, we see displays of leadership, the denial of pain in self or others, competitiveness, a fascination with rules, the restful dualism of winning and losing, the excitement of physical contact, and, often, that provocative male dichotomy of nudity and armor. The language of athletics always brings American conversation to a level playing field.

Still, in academe, where the athlete is often used for glory and fund-raising, the attitude is complex and, at times, cynical. The Greek ideal of the scholar-athlete jostles with the general contempt for the "dumb jock." The trouble with academicians is you can never

9

be 100 percent sure how much they really like sports. After all, on *their* state occasions, they wear a form of dress and a helmet seemingly designed only for protection from bird droppings.

Attendance

At root, *attendance* means paying attention as well as being there. Showing up, however, has always taken precedence in our society over the quality of one's work while present. Both schools and industry are trying to shift the emphasis from mere presence to performance.

Both sectors raise the question as to whether rewards for good attendance are effective. Skeptics of whatever occupational stripe ask, "Why should someone be rewarded merely for complying with a fundamental expectation?"

Yet another point of similarity: the phrase "attendance problem" in both business and education is used interchangeably with the phrase "absenteeism problem." Attendance, of course, is *not* the problem, but it does sound more positive. Thus, while equally unsuccessful in resolving the dilemma of no-shows, both business and education find solace in doublethink.

Attitude

This word means the same in both worlds, but business uses it less frequently. The acceptable business substitute for having a good attitude is being a team player.

Even in the classroom, teachers are more likely to replace what they once termed having a good attitude with being conscientious, positive, or eager, and to admonish the old-fashioned bad attitude as "inappropriate behavior."

Inappropriate, by the way, fundamentally means not belonging, not fitting in. As is often the case, we speak truer than we mean to. Appearance, in school, work, and society, is as important as appearing. Perhaps it's no accident that attitude is also a pose.

Discussion Questions

1. How can the differences between Accountability and Responsibility, as described in chapter A, characterize the differences between business and education?

2. How can the differences between Appraisal and Evaluation do
   the same?
3. To what extent does business seem to be adapting attitudes
   characteristic of education and education of business?
4. How could such a switch be explained?
5. What evidence is there to suggest that outside of academe,
   thoughts and ideas are considered unreal and/or unimportant in
   our culture?
6. What obstacles or limitations do schools encounter in motivating performance that business does not?

Looking Ahead

To continue the discussion of performance appraisal in business and education, see "Of Teacher Evaluation and Teachers' Evaluations" at the end of
chapter E.

B is Bottom Line

Benchmarking

This relatively new business practice refers to the identification, analysis, and measurement of a company, program, department, function, and so on, that is so outstanding as to serve as a model or benchmark for other businesses to emulate. The academic analog to a business benchmark goes by such names as model, standard-bearer, or showcase school.

While showcase schools are set up in advance as experiments to test new paths for others, business benchmarks begin with the same purpose as all business enterprises. They become benchmarks only after they've proved profitable.

In the business world, the general process of imitation goes by such names as competitiveness or market research. Not only is it the sincerest flattery, it's the road to success. In academe, this is called plagiarism or cheating. Academic imitations are labeled unoriginal or derivative. In business, they are described as improved, synergized, or enhanced.

Best of Class

"Best of class" seems to come from the school domain but was really created by and for business. The best-of-class distinction refers to a model, standard, benchmark, or paradigm other businesses might choose to imitate. (See Benchmarking.)

It's hard to imagine a contemporary educator using such an expression, despite the schoolhouse phraseology. *Best* is a word dangerously incompatible with today's correct social attitudes. One must be very careful about making judgments based on comparisons. A teacher might risk saying, in low-key fashion, "She's the best student in my class," but the limits of the praise are strongly implied.

Though *best* is a superlative, then, and a potential absolute, "of class" clarifies that the standard is still safely relative: best of its kind or type compared to the others. It's not the bold assertion of absolute excellence it may first strike the ear as being.

Bottom Line

This is the only absolute; everything else is relative. The bottom line is an abstract with an implied life and volition of its own. "Personally, I don't want to do thus and so, but the bottom line says I must." In education, the ultimate absolute that dictates harsh decisions is called the budget. Business is leading the way in exploring the concept that the bottom line might, after all, bear some relationship to quality or delivery.

Whether or not schools have bottom lines is a topic under debate. The question gains emotional intensity to the degree that all value is equated with bottom lines.

In general speech, "bottom line" means the synopsis or ultimate outcome. Our culture equates the net profit with the essence of all.

Bureaucracy

In government, education, or business, a bureaucracy is a system of entrenched, unimaginative people characterized by a love of formality, complexity, and consistency for their own sakes. *Policy, code, procedure,* and *regulation* are key bureaucratic nouns; *comply,* the key verb. Historically, bureaucracies are named only to be denounced.

The development of bureaucracies is a part of the evolutionary process of all human systems; they meet a constant need of one aspect of the composite human personality. We hate them because they resist change and value them for precisely the same reason. They block and save us from our true selves.

13

Business

Business always means "serious." Making money is no laughing matter. (See Humor.) Teachers may tell their students to get down to business. That means something like "wake up and smell the coffee."

In the business world, to say "I think we can do business" means "I think we speak the same language and share the same ground rules and assumptions." It's not easy for schools and business to do business.

"To mean business" is also equated with getting the job done. In times of weariness with process, the myth of businessman-as-hero always surfaces with renewed popularity. Consider Lee Iacocca, H. Ross Perot.

Busyness

Nobody uses this word at all any more, but the etymological core of *business* should never be forgotten. At the deepest level of the business consciousness (or unconsciousness) is a faith in the virtue of activity, the condition of being busy. One has a can-do attitude and then one *does*. Any appearance of inactivity is eschewed for its resemblance to death.

Buy-In

While *best of class* sounds educational but is a business coinage, *buy-in* sounds businesslike, but comes from popular counterculture. Teachers and businesspersons are equally comfortable with the term that equates commitment, concurrence, or agreement with monetary investment. (See Ownership.)

✦ ✦ ✦

Can/Do/Think

Are thought and action mutually exclusive? Common everyday experience says no. Everything in our culture says yes. Is one of these alleged poles better? Again our culture's answer is yes. American society has always chosen the man of action. (Actions speak louder than words. He thinks too much; such men are dangerous. Idleness is the tool of the devil. Let us, then, be up and doing.)

There is no question that our culture applauds busyness, while ever striving to produce greater leisure. Why else are holiday greetings, newsletters, and mandatory monthly reports generally lists of the things we have done? Our existence in the universe is justified by busyness. If only there is enough activity, we seem to feel, no one will ask what it means. The most expedient way to throw dust in the air is to keep running. The idea of measuring activity in reference to defined purposes, goals, and objectives is still being preached as a new concept in the busi-ness world, and our proverbs and habits of mind and action have certainly not caught up with an MBO (management-by-objectives) outlook.

Busyness is reinforced by our responses to the seasons of nature, upon which agricultural activities and the school calendar are based. Fall is the busy get-serious-and-prepare-for-privation season; spring is the busy wind-up-and-get-ready-for-summer one. Summer is busy because there are so many daylight hours for work and play; winter is busy because there are so few. Winter is also busy because people dread idleness. How sad to lose that golden time for dreaming by the fire.

Busyness is likewise inherent in the cycles and evolution of business. We are happily overbusy when business is good. (In shops and restau-rants, a busy day is a good, profitable day.) During downturns and bad times, we lay off people and have to hustle. That's why lean, despite our love of all things "lite," is mean. Who wouldn't feel mean when they have to work two-and-a-half jobs? Our labor-saving technological advances have proved deceptive. Yes, they are labor saving in that they replace individuals in the labor force, but they are also labor generating in (al-most) enabling one person to do the work and experience the pressures of several. Thanks to something as simple and common as the answering machine, we can be out and in at the same time, being literally answer-able for twice the work volume. Thanks to cellular phones, we never escape.

Contrary to the habitual opposition of thinking and doing, creative and imaginative people are especially prone to overbusyness because they can always see further possibilities in anything they undertake. The unimaginative (alas, the majority by the time they reach adulthood) are the ones who need to be kept busy as a preferable alternative to drugs and crime sprees. Yet it is also true that too much busyness gets in the way of imagination. Idleness (and the timeless, right-brain mode) is the stuff daydreams are made on, while busyness is the tool of conformity. (The less we ponder, the more we can fit in, and vice versa.) Perhaps, indeed, that is why it is possible to succeed in busyness without really trying—and why skillful imitators are usually first in the business compe-tition for speed of delivery.

But if doing is number one in this dichotomy, where does teaching fit in? That is clear: "Those who can, do. Those who can't, teach." This certainly says where teaching ranks in our culture. Rankly and grossly, of course.

Yet, there *is* a solid core of truth to this saying, and it's not even an insult to teachers. Knowing how to do something is, in fact, not the same as knowing how to teach something. They are completely different skills; some people have one or the other, and some have both. Further, it clearly is not necessary to be able to do something in order to coach, teach, or critique it. Still, this is not what people mean when they quote the expression. They mean teachers are people who have flunked out of life.

In the olden days, of course, people used to be smarter. In the Middle Ages, for instance, they had the opportunity of enlisting for either the active or the contemplative life, because the church valued both. And the Renaissance ideal was a balance of thinking and doing. Still, the cult of busyness for its own sake has also always existed for those who fear the Void.

Indeed, at the end of the sixteenth century, Montaigne told how, in ancient times, Aesop observed his master void while walking, explaining it was to save time. The fablist's conjecture as to what body function must next be performed on the run we shall politely leave to the reader's imagination—or to a glance at Montaigne's "Of Experience."

Discussion Questions

1. Is the bottom line in the financial sense really the bottom line in the common sense of essence or core meaning? What kinds of people would say that it is, and what would be their reasons? What kinds of people would say that it isn't, and what would be their reasons?
2. What evidence is there to suggest that outside of academe, thoughts and ideas are considered unreal and/or unimportant in our culture? Do you agree?

C is Competitive Can-Do

Canon

Canon originally applied to church dogma, officially approved books of the Bible, and the core of the Mass (*Webster's Ninth New Collegiate Dictionary*). In academe, it is nearly as important, referring to a list of the most significant works, chiefly literary, that are considered essential to a basic education. Most who object to the traditional canon say it fails to represent the experiences and perceptions of females and minorities. Some objections center on specific moral and religious issues. Given the limitations of time, competition for a place in the canon is as intense as it would be in any zero-sum game.

The conflict over the canon is analogous to the time of corporate crisis when a company reconsiders what business it is in, determines its mission and product lines, and affirms the identity of its customers. A unique problem for educators is that, apart from religious conservatives, few outside of academe feel the lack of an official literary canon as a problem. The word *canon* itself does not occur in business. However, a loose cannon is one who uses power, energy, and ambition without official sanction.

✦ ✦ ✦

Is versus *Ought*

Underlying the dispute about the canon is the question, do we want schools to be change agents for society as well as for individuals? The argument is probably most intense in the world of higher education, where passions over subject matter run especially deep.

Is this debate merely academic? The continuing battle over possession of the canon is a distinct campaign in our ongoing culture wars. Social questions at issue are

- *To what extent does the teaching of history perpetuate "wrong" attitudes and obstruct necessary change?*
- *To what extent is education about what was and is, and to what extent is it about what should be?*
- *How can we maintain a common cultural heritage if the canon is no longer based on historical significance?*
- *Do we need a common cultural heritage and language in a global society?*
- *Why teach the past at all when there is so much new learning to acquire?*
- *Who cares? (And why?)*

✦ ✦ ✦

Career

At its source, the word ca*reer* has to do with a racecourse or running. Thus, it carries with it the idea that life is a competition along a straight and predictable trajectory. The corporate world increasingly acknowledges a variety of career tracks (note we're still in the racecourse metaphor), some of which admittedly lead nowhere.

The good thing about teaching young people to think in terms of careers is that it fosters the ideas of sequential thinking, projection into the future, and the consideration of consequences. As such, it's a useful corrective to the fragmented, moment-to-moment value system they habitually inhabit. It also encourages the healthful notion that one creates and shapes one's own life through a combination of planning, effort, and thought. The bad thing is this isn't necessarily so.

Challenge

Challenge is a positive business noun for something hard that one encounters. One never gives up doing—unless one's last act is to pull the

19

plug. *Challenge* is a positive education verb for *making* something hard. One challenges students to foster learning.

In both arenas, difficulty is seen as an adversary—perhaps created as part of a cosmic lesson plan—against which one competes. It's a way of treating life as a game.

Change

The business world continually cites ever-accelerating change as a major stress—or challenge. In schools, change has been proposed, along with future studies, as an important area of study for the last twenty years. That particular change has been slow in coming.

Businesspeople who regard themselves as change agents often point out how difficult it is to effect corporate change or a change of culture. Teachers have always been change agents: their desired end result (or output) is change or growth in the student. They already know it's hard to produce.

Changes in organization or technique in both worlds are called innovations when they work, and fads when they don't.

Choice

Proponents of school choice mean different things by the term. Their basic premise, though, equates education and consumerism. They believe the movement of children from one institution to another will both reflect and determine which ones thrive, producing a kind of market-driven, quality education.

Choice, as in freedom of choice, can be only a positive word for Americans. Those who object to, or have reservations about, this type of school choice are unlikely to get a favorable hearing until they find an equally positive name for their position.

Except when making recommendations about school reform, business leaders are notably reticent about choices and choosing. The business term for making choices is *decision making*. (See Decision Making.) Decision making is a more forceful, active process, often involving taking initiative and giving direction. Choosing suggests selecting within a limited, predetermined field. One offers choices to customers, children, and spouses; top executives make decisions.

Choice Implications

School-choice advocates believe at least some of the following:

- *Competition yields excellence.*
- *Educators have a profit mentality.*
- *Teachers and administrators adjust their performance in order to acquire funds.*
- *Schools and businesses improve as financial and community support is withdrawn and they head toward bankruptcy.*
- *Schools that close will be replaced by something better serving all the same students.*
- *Everyone has resources to relocate their children.*
- *It doesn't matter that not everyone could relocate children.*

School-choice opponents believe at least some of the following:

- *Schools exist to serve a public need.*
- *Interest in the effectiveness of the school goes beyond the interests of individual children and families; otherwise childless people would not also support schools.*
- *Pulling the plug on a school does not punish ineffective or greedy "owners"; it hurts the common good.*
- *Transferring public funding to private institutions will spread the ills of public schools to the private sector.*
- *There are sound philosophical reasons for the distinction between public and private.*
- *School-choice proposals are more advantageous to those who already have more advantages.*
- *We already have school choice in this country.*

Something about the topic of school choice seems, in fact, to inspire an analysis of underlying beliefs and motives. For example, David Thornburg produced a similar analysis of the case made by advocates in a similar format. (See his *Edutrends 2000: Restructuring, Technology, and the Future of Education.*) In like manner, Tom Watkins examined underlying beliefs of "zealots and ideologues" whose motives undermine support for the charter school option. (See "So You Want to Start a Charter School?" *Education Week*, Sept. 6, 1995.)

Cognition, Cognitive

These are education terms for higher intellectual functioning. They never occur in business.

Committee

Committee is, by now, a somewhat old-fashioned term for a group of people working together. Long fabled for their ineffectualness, committees have been supplanted in business by teams, task forces, and, for a time, quality circles. Business committees nowadays tend to serve only such frivolous functions as affording hospitality or sunshine. While teams and task forces exist to accomplish a purpose, committees and circles suggest an enjoyment of group process for its own sake. Teams have leaders; committees merely have chairs—the image suggests they sit around going nowhere.

Among educators, the committee is not so out of favor. Academic committees, for example, are still considered honorable. Indeed, a proposed name change to academic team would probably be considered trivial, if not demeaning. Chairs are honorable. Often they are even endowed.

Communication

Business, government, the military, education, and the general public all agree that the art of communication is important. In the name of communication, we persuade, give orders, influence, indoctrinate, even educate. Lack of foresight or forthrightness is often called lack of communication.

Few words are positive, neutral, and deceptive at once. This is.

Compensation

In business, compensation refers to the reward one receives in exchange for work, contribution, performance.

In education, it means pretty much the same things. It also refers to something one does to make up for a failure, disadvantage, shortcoming, or lack.

Business thinks in terms of gain; educators, in terms of balance.

Compensatory

Compensatory education programs are designed to offset disadvantages caused by such social factors as poverty, discrimination, or nonmainstream cultures and lifestyles. In a business setting, this might be called reasonable accommodation. The business community generally fears the extension of mandated accommodation. Educators are used to being accommodating. (See Reasonable, Reasonable Accommodation.)

Competence, Competency, Core Competencies

In both business and education, the word *competence* is usually reserved for the minimal level of functioning—just as in the legal world, to be competent to stand trial does not call for a very high standard of performance.

Competencies are the specific components—the skills, attitudes, principles—that make up this general competence to work or sustain life (*Dictionary of Education*). The word has a distinctly practical orientation. In educational circles, the notion of competencies is usually linked to job or occupational training.

Businesses engaged in restructuring or re-engineering often spell out the basic or core competencies needed to function in new or evolving capacities within the organization. (See Restructuring [and Re-engineering].) In some cases, the term is used for high-level positions as well as low-level ones. Core competencies are the closest equivalent in business to the academic curriculum.

Competition, A Competition

It is a fundamental American belief that competition (in its most abstract form, without an article) is a good thing. Our society doesn't really believe in self-starters or in a reward system without a one-up component. Stimulation, it is believed, depends on an outside threat.

For these reasons, one of the first things business leaders involved in school reform advocate is school choice. The notion of a good, excellent, or better school in the absence of external competition is inconceivable. How, after all, can you know what you're *for* if you don't first know what you're *against?* This is the perpetual position of those who lack ideas.

A competition is a contest, with rules, with the intent to produce a winner, and with an implication of fairness. Both business and education use them as motivators (external stimuli) for employees or students.

The Competition

The business technique for countering fear and its dreaded debilitation

(the annihilation of busy-ness) is to call distressing forms of competition, "*the* competition," a term that instantly elevates the source of fear into a depersonalized enemy without a name. This linguistic maneuver brings that liberation from rules that the war metaphor always implies and gives one the courage of battle adrenaline. (See Metaphor.) Making battle (or game) plans against the competition seems easier and less threatening than designing, building, marketing, and selling a better mousetrap.

The lurking war metaphor may also be a reason for the lowered enthusiasm for competition in school settings—"we're trying to civilize" goes the thinking, "and competition always threatens to get out of hand." Traditional private schools, to be sure, are skilled in the deliberate management of competition, having been allied with business interests for generations. Schools advocating development of the whole child, however, are not convinced of the value of an atmosphere of competition. (See Cooperation, Cooperative Learning.) For one thing, it encourages cheating.

Competition—Domestic/Foreign/Global

Foreign, global, and some kinds of domestic competition are forms of competition that threaten to exceed the comfort level—stimulating, perhaps, but also frightening. The word *global* lends an undeniable grandeur to the company that has to face up to this new war of the worlds. It magnifies the threat. *Foreign* connotes unfairness and an unsportsmanslike conduct alien to our culture. It sneers at the adversary. Manageable domestic competition, in contrast, may be referred to, with an almost friendly familiarity, as "our competition." The term implies, "*We* know what they're up to!"

Competitive

In business, this means "in the running," and it's high praise. In schools, it often means "making trouble." Children must learn to get along.

24

Compulsory Education

The earliest American schooling requirements were that every child be able to read and write by a certain age (usually twelve) and that jurisdictions of a specified size provide teachers to serve the community (*Dictionary of Education*). Later, the requirement was changed to mean that children under the age of sixteen must attend school, whether they learn anything or not.

This evolution has gone in the opposite direction from business, which used to put more emphasis on making sure that workers punched in and out as required, but now is considering that time served is less significant than the satisfaction of objectives.

What business calls management by objectives and educators call (among other things) mastery learning was law in the seventeenth century.

Concern

In education, to say, "I have a concern about . . . " is a professionally detached way of saying, "I'm worried about" something or someone. For academics, merely recognizing problems, especially in advance, confers prestige; to express or communicate a problem within the community is often considered a form of action sufficient in and of itself.

Concern is never used in this sense in business, where its meaning is always positive. A concern is a portion that one owns, would like to own, or is considering owning. One never has a concern about, but only a concern in. A "going concern" is an enterprise that is thriving. In both arenas, a concern may imply a stake in, though educators consider it unprofessional to suggest much personal interest. (See Interest.)

Concerns as problems or worries do not exist in business. Such things become challenges, or a competitive call to corrective action. If no action is intended or possible, the subject is not raised.

Conformity

The word *conformity* is not used at all in business and is mentioned only to be denied or decried in education. Like the God of the Old Testament, it is too potent a value ever to be named directly. (Cf. Attitude; Obedience; Socialization; Team Player.)

25

Continuous Improvement

Continuous improvement, popular in business, is an ill-fitting notion for education. Growth and learning don't happen continuously; they happen in spurts. Important, mysterious things often happen on a plateau or even in a backslide. It is not unusual to learn of progress that occurred years after the actual work was done.

Like medieval laborers, teachers often don't live to see the final cathedral they've helped erect. This timing problem complicates evaluation.

Cooperation, Cooperative Learning

Cooperation means working together. Business has many names for group effort in solving common problems or achieving common goals, but *cooperation* and *cooperative*, perhaps tainted by socialist and schoolroom connotations, are not among them. Far preferable to the corporate ear are teamwork, win-win, and alliances, which come from the sports arena or theaters of war.

In the schoolroom, cooperation can refer to compliance with authority and conflict avoidance or to group effort.

The beliefs that the combination of group goals and individual accountability improves learning and that the educational whole is often greater than the sum of its parts, according to Arthur Ellis and Jeffrey Fouts (*Research on Educational Innovations*, pp. 122-23), are key in the many variations on cooperative learning. Observation and research support these beliefs, which in the business world are heralded as synergy. Ellis and Fouts also note that most educators have found cooperative learning effective in offsetting the limitations of individualistic and competitive approaches to learning (p. 120).

Nevertheless, Americans remain convinced that solitary competition works best and most accords with the real world. It goes against our grain to imitate Confucian harmony, even if it's good for us. (See Robin Barrow and Geoffrey Milburn, *A Critical Dictionary of Educational Concepts*, 2d ed., pp. 57–59, and Alfie Kohn, *No Contest: The Case Against Competition*, rev. ed.)

Co-ops

Cooperative education, cooperative programs, or, most simply, co-ops are arrangements by which students receive part of their training at a participating, "real-world" workplace.

The appeal of co-ops to students is that they provide real-world experience, useful in getting a job. (See Real World.) The appeal to business management is that they provide a low-cost way to train and try out prospective employees without recruiting them and to fill vacancies created by layoffs and hiring freezes. They're a source of cheap help.

Creativity

Creativity is appreciated more in the abstract than in everyday life. Most people find actual creativity puzzling and marginally threatening. It's a different way of thinking, too unpredictable for comfort. In education, the word is often trivialized and equated with cut-and-paste projects or alleged self-expression. In business, a creative solution can be a euphemism for a devious one, a clever stratagem (as in creative accounting). In short, the drive is to reduce creativity to the predictable and the familiar.

Educators have long wondered what business is also starting to investigate: is there a way creativity can be taught? More creativity-training packages appear on the market shelves almost daily.

Cross Training

Cross training in business gives employees the knowledge and skills to perform other jobs or serve other functions within the same organization. Traditionally, an employee with outdated skills would simply be fired and replaced with someone who had the new necessary skills.

The practices of retraining and cross training presuppose that learning is a continuing process, that adults retain the ability to learn, and that schools produce graduates who are teachable, rather than finished products to be slotted into positions that exist at the time of their graduation. These are useful considerations when schools are attacked for failing to teach specific job skills.

Culture

The concept of culture has a long history in education and a short one in business. Like many terms dear to the teaching profession, it has an agrarian origin, referring to cultivation and growth or tillage of the soil. (See Metaphor.)

One of the prime historic purposes of education has always been the preservation and transmission of the values and traditions of the society it serves. Appreciation requires a certain mental growth (the *cultivation* of taste) within the students. Some students find this effort broadening, and others, alienating.

Meanwhile, businesses turning inward and pondering change have taken to viewing their own values, traditions, norms, and rules as unique corporate cultures. It makes a company's way of doing things sound instantly better—almost like having good taste.

Curriculum, Curriculum Vitae

The curriculum of an educational institution or program is the set of courses or subjects presented for study, usually including the learning required for a degree or certification (*Dictionary of Education*).

Like the words *career* and *course*, *curriculum* derives from the Latin for running. When educators aren't cultivating growth, they're training runners for the racetrack of life, or curriculum vitae.

Curriculum vitae, incidentally, is the name academics give to résumés. (For curricular issues, see Canon; Hierarchy in Education; Integrity, Academic Integrity, Integrated Curriculum, Integral.)

Customer, Customer Service

At root, a customer is one *accustomed* to purchase a certain service or product; one who frequents a particular place of business on a regular or systematic basis. By definition, a customer is governed by habit; an habitué.

American business, having long grown accustomed to the faces of its customers, was shocked to discover in the last quarter of this century that it was taking these habitual spenders too much for granted. As a corrective, it invented the new concept of customer service, which, of course, used to be simply a part of being in business. Now it is introduced to eager trainees who ply it with conspicuous and often intrusive zeal.

Customize, Individualize

To customize means to modify in such a way as to meet, or appear to meet, individual needs and wishes of customers or to accommodate individual differences. It is a form of customer service.

In education, customizing is called individualizing. This adaptation to individual needs and learning styles has been a recommended, if not mandated, aspect of the teacher's toolbox for at least a generation. One-room schoolhouses used the technique (as well as self-paced learning) all

28

along, before they were displaced by the school-as-factory model, to meet the needs of the then new workforce.

✦ ✦ ✦

The Broken Analogy: Students in the Factory Model

The analogy between our schools and the industrial-age factory seems too familiar to repeat. It has been drawn many times—facetiously, maliciously, humorously, indignantly, and, doubtless at some point, earnestly, as a matter of pride.

Like most long-accepted analogies, it has much truth in it. Nineteenth-century schools did become efficient models of industrialism. Students, as much as possible, were converted into uniform, interchangeable units for batch processing, grouped according to age, and taught by a series of specialists in fragmented disciplines. Bells rang at uniform intervals to announce when it was time for the line to progress; the production schedule ran from September to June; and the raw material, which entered at age five, emerged as finished products at age eighteen. According to this profile, the finished products were obedient, passive industrial workers, themselves interchangeable units, who could be trained to repeat a fragmented task according to the production schedule.

Critics of our schools say the world has changed and business has changed with it. We need new skills and new models to prepare for the information age. Schools better "get with the program"; they need to change in parallel ways.

But as long as we're pausing to question, why not also question our analogy? Are schools really miserably failed businesses, just as women since the time of Aristotle were considered miserably failed (incompletely processed) men? Let us look again at the comparison of businesses and schools, starting with organization:

Business	Public School	Private School
Stockholders	Taxpayers	Parents (tuition payers)
Board of directors	School board	Trustees
CEO	Superintendent	Headmaster/ mistress

29

Business	Public School	Private School
Vice presidents	Principals	Division heads, Directors
Directors	Asst principals	Deans
Managers, Department heads	Department heads	Department heads

So far, so good. But now what? Are teachers the supervisors and students the workers? Are teachers the workers and students the product? Are students the raw material . . . or the consumers? Are they the market? What *are* the students, besides a monkey wrench in the whole system?

And what is the product, or service, of a school? A good citizen? A good worker? A good learner? An education? A diploma? An experience? When do you know you've met your objective? After a test? At the end of a term? At graduation time? When the student gets a job or is accepted into a program or other school? Two years after a course is over? Twenty years? How can you work long-term student/teacher performance appraisal into a strategic plan? When are the results really in?

Looking at the analogy this closely, taking the figure of speech literally, as more and more people are doing, suddenly all the hot spots in school reform seem to center at the point where the analogy breaks down.

Those who believe students and/or parents are consumers or customers stress school choice and market-driven curriculum designs and teaching styles. They believe poorly run schools deserve to go out of business, discounting the notion that schools exist to serve the public good, not to make a profit for individuals.

Those who believe students are the product and teachers are the workers stress testing and merit pay. Measure teacher performance, they say, by measuring their output (what students learn), reward the top performers and punish or dismiss the rest. Though introduced in the context of our information-age debate, these views still uphold the old industrial-age analogy.

Those who believe students are the workers and teachers are their supervisors want to assess teachers as motivators, managers, and influencers, ultimately responsible for the quality of their workers' output.

It might be helpful to note some of the following differences between workers and students. Then consider what it means to manage each group. Workers are selected and placed by qualification to fill a job or position (that is, the person is chosen to match the job). They work voluntarily, are paid directly for work they perform, and they usually can be discharged at will. They are adults. Students in most public schools undergo no selection process. The job or position is designed to some extent to match the person (i.e., the job is modified to suit the existing abilities of the student). They work as required or mandated by law (involuntarily), they pay indirectly through parent taxes or tuition to work, and they are rarely discharged. Usually, they are children. Public school students, in effect, combine the qualities of slaves or forced laborers and consumers paying for a service to which, in another sense, they are also entitled. Curious.

Each of these analogies, then, has some serious flaws. No wonder business leaders often think educators overcomplicate things. No wonder educators often think business oversimplifies them. We'll do our best to track these and other conundrums as we go along. Perhaps the beginning of understanding lies just in asking questions.

Discussion Questions

1. What linguistic evidence shows that our culture generally views life as a competitive sport or game?
2. What does this basic comparison imply about motivation? Attitudes toward others? How goals or values are established/set? Our measures of success?
3. Review Athlete. What is the significance of the athlete for our culture?

For Further Consideration

1. How do you learn best? Working alone for a personally established purpose (e.g., to make my ideal lamp)? Working alone to defeat competition (to make a lamp that's better than Harry's)? Working with others for a mutually established purpose? Working with others to defeat competition?
2. Which ways of learning do you enjoy most and why?
3. Locate some people who answer these questions differently and find out how their choices work for them.

31

Looking Ahead

To continue the discussion of competition and teamwork in business and education, see Team; Team Building; Team Performance (Evaluation and Reward); Team Player; Team Teaching (and Self-Managed Teams).

D: Discipline or Diversity?

Decision Making

Decision making means completely different things in the two worlds.

For top executives, skill in decision making has long been a source of pride. With empowerment, however, the people lower in business organizations are supposed to make decisions. Top executives must now think strategically. That seems harder.

For educators, decision making refers not to power but to morality and moral education. It has nothing to do with looking outward, giving or carrying out orders, and everything to do with looking inward and directing the self. Those who see a moral decline in our society say that's precisely what is wrong with it. (See Values Clarification; Moral Education, Morality, Moral Reasoning.)

Delegation

Delegation in business is the assignment to others of work for which they are held accountable. In education, delegation is a group of people who claim to represent others in lodging a complaint or making a demand.

Demand

In economics, demand is the desire to purchase a product or service combined with the ability and willingness to pay for it (*McGraw-Hill Dictionary of Modern Economics,* 3d ed.). In politics and education, it is a desire that is often unaccompanied by the ability or willingness to pay.

Demographics

This branch of learning begins with the statistical study of the population, including distribution, vital statistics, and capacity for growth or decline (*Webster's Ninth New Collegiate Dictionary*). In democracies and market-driven economies like ours, this information is essential to planning, and all of our institutions rely on it heavily. The objective is to spot a bandwagon while people are still hitching up the team and build a road in the direction it seems to be heading. It is often a very effective substitute for thought and conviction.

Development

Development as an activity or area of corporate responsibility always refers to the advancement of skills, knowledge, and perhaps professional standing of employees. Thus we have training and development (T&D), human resource development (HRD), research and development (R&D), and organization development (OD). Development in business involves learning.

In colleges, universities, and private schools, development (as in Office of Development) refers primarily to raising money. (See Marketing.)

Developmental, Stages of Development

Educators do sometimes use the word *development* to pertain to something educational, as in stages of development, but for the most part, the forms of the word they reserve for educational usage are the verb *develop*, the adjective *developmental*, or the increasingly necessary adverb, *developmentally*.

These terms are crucial and venerable in education, while only just entering into business. The reason for the difference is that education, by definition, is concerned with human change and growth and thus relies heavily on the findings of developmental psychology. Business, on the other hand, has until recently assumed that its human component (adults)

34

was already "grown up" and had no farther to go. Those at the higher echelons may still be in the habit of viewing themselves in that light.

Disability

In business, a disability has always been a condition that prevents one from working at all or from working in a position held before illness or accident struck. In education, it's a condition that doesn't prevent working (learning), but that makes it harder or calls for different teaching and studying techniques. It's also the raw material teachers generally work with. Under the Americans with Disabilities Act, it is coming to mean the same thing in business. (See Reasonable, Reasonable Accommodation.)

Discipline

There are academic circles in which the word *discipline* has retained its original meaning—a field of study, an area one teaches. More prevalent, though, in both business and education is the doublethink meaning of discipline. Just as discussions of attendance are really about the opposite of attendance (absenteeism), so-called discipline problems come from a *lack* of discipline (or training). Discipline in both domains has also come to mean a specific approach to training—namely, the use of punishment to change behavior.

Both schools and business use progressive discipline, a legalistic system of warnings and consequences designed above all to protect the organization from lawsuits, and both institutions periodically make pronouncements and have training sessions emphasizing that discipline is not punishing, but teaching. Their impact tends to be short-lived.

✦ ✦ ✦
One Dean's Aphorisms on Discipline

1. Discipline is not a good in and of itself; the only discipline that is meaningful is self-discipline, and that is of value only insofar as it serves a worthy end.
2. The fewer rules, the better. If limited to only a few rules, one is obliged to make them express values. (Consider Hammurabi's Code, Moses's ten, Christ's two.)
3. Any rule that can be maintained only through a system of punishments is a bad (i.e., unnecessary) rule.

4. Overdependency on punishment diverts thought from values. Ends and means become confused, since punishment, intended as a means, appears as an evil, or end. This is not conducive to the development of moral reasoning.

5. Punishments are symbolic, asserting the community's values. Their purpose is not to change behavior, for that rarely happens.

6. The weaker the internal restraints, the stronger the need for external ones; the stronger the external restraints, the weaker the development of self-control.

7. To try to instill obedience for its own sake is not productive in our posthierarchical times. Civilization's only hope is in developing the ability to reason. This requires dialogue.

8. The world is divided between those who think justice means treating everyone the same and those who think that justice means adjusting for individual differences. That is why every judicial decision is followed by a great outcry and why it is useless to worry about pleasing the public.

9. In a high-achievement environment, people would learn more if failure, mediocrity, and irrelevance were tolerated instead of punished.

10. The more concerned an institution is with precedents, policies, and procedures, the stronger the reason to suspect it lacks values.

✦ ✦ ✦

Diversity, Managing Diversity, Valuing Diversity

Once a broad abstraction, *diversity* has become a shortcut reference to the varied, majority-lacking population and workforce we foresee for the next century. It signals a desire to view differences among human beings in a new, positive light, to tap into the new energy of thinking global instead of fearing foreign.

The popular business phrase "managing diversity" may, however, betray some national doubt about our future. According to the expression, one does not manage people or individuals, but an abstract quality they are thought collectively to possess—diversity. Are we dehumanizing the very people we secretly fear and dislike? And is diversity something one controls or limits, that one handles or copes with, that one endures with grudging resignation while secretly hoping it, too, will pass? The ever-ambiguous term *managing* suggests some of each.

Valuing diversity, in contrast, is a clear affirmation, though the hypersensitive might quibble, if they choose, about a possibly patronizing implication.

While business wrestles with glass ceilings, affirmative action, the specter of quotas, and questions of management style, schools agonize over bilingual education, the canon, and defining the core curriculum. These are difficult issues that require thought, openness, goodwill, and trust. Business and education have no precedents for using these qualities on such a scale.

Downsizing

Out of a crowded field of candidates, *downsizing* has become the preferred word for a reduction in the number of employees. It's a clean, neutral, and proactive-sounding expression for what is often a decision born of fear.

Dress Codes

Our culture is ambivalent about dress codes, so it's not always easy to tell what is the leading edge. In the business world, the relaxed blue-jean environment of a Ben & Jerry's is considered progressive, whereas public schools that demand conformity to a code are heralded as revolutionary. Boarding schools (which prepare the privileged for business and political leadership) have always had dress codes and private day schools, uniforms; there, it would be revolutionary to dispense with the code. (See "Uniform Lessons for Life" at the end of chap. R.)

The immature regard dress codes as infringements of liberty and identity; the more mature buy books and take seminars to master the art of disguise (dressing for success through power colors, power ties, power shoes, etc.). The most mature regard dress as mere convention and often prefer avoiding the whole issue by working at home in jogging clothes or bathrobes.

There are voluminous records of disputes and arbitrations about which dress (and style) requirements in business are legitimate and which violate fundamental rights. Written codes can be tyrannical; unwritten and unspoken ones, more so.

Women's apparel seems most resistant to regulation since women don't have a uniform equivalent to the male coat and tie. Women also have the responsibility of judging the line between *gender* and *sex*, words which though often used interchangeably, are anything but synonymous.

Male facial hair has also presented a workplace legal thicket, in which industrial hygienists must testify as to the impact of whiskers on health, safety, and job performance. The meaning of a beard or mustache varies with one's rank, position, or role in an organization. Facial hair generally inspires confidence in outside consultants, distrust of upper management, fellowship with middle management, and disgust at workers. In schools, where it symbolizes maturity, common practice is to allow it on teachers and prohibit it on students.

Japanese manufacturers circumvent the problems of a code by having one uniform for all. In America, freedom of expression is rarely enhanced by the dictum, "Do as you please." Told to do as they please, most people are at a loss and quickly look for someone to imitate. Americans prefer to conform by choice.

Dress Code Questions for Educators

1. Are we preparing the young for society as it is or as it ought to be?

D   D: Discipline or Diversity?

2. Is there a specific rank or role in society that our code is designed to support?
3. Is appearance important?
4. How much emphasis should be put on appearance?
5. Do we control behavior by controlling appearance?
6. How much time and energy are we as educators prepared to invest in maintaining appearance?
7. What is our desired end result and is that served or harmed by a system of specific dress rules?
8. Do we want to help parents resist pressure to overspend on clothes or is that beyond our social responsibility?

Drill

Drill is systematic repetition designed to master a skill or body of information (*Dictionary of Education*). Many complain that it is boring. To bore, of course, is the purpose of a drill. It is an effective and useful exercise that is well named. One needn't like everything that works.

-Driven

Is the business world manly, mighty, decisive? Or is it made up of wimps in wolves' clothing? This fashionable suffix suggests both. Everything is *something*-driven. Business language is steeped in images of drive, aggression, and power; the love of the combustion engine dies hard, as does the vision of the commander shouting orders above the roar of winds and engines. Yet, who really is calling the shots? We are market-driven, customer-driven, budget-driven, even, some say, integrity-driven. Could there be some teflon on the shaft or pusillanimity in the piston?

Of course, one doesn't hear of anything being *-driven* in academe, whose practitioners never claim to be in the driver's seat. Educators have always unabashedly acknowledged that there are tides (even) in the affairs of man. Their pride is in detecting winds and currents.

Dyslexia

Dyslexia is the best-known type of learning disability. It is a linguistic deficiency that impairs a person's ability to read, spell, organize, and remember words. Like persons with other kinds of learning disabilities, dyslexics are often quite successful once they escape from school.

Spellcheck, audiotapes, secretaries, assistants, and editors all enable them to function fine in the real world. They can be especially good at running things because while others were learning the fundamental skills in school, they were cultivating personality and learning to read subtle signals given off by other people. These are the basics of political acumen. (See Politics.)

◆ ◆ ◆

Of Rules, Humor, and Learning

As a young child, I was very anxious about the rules. I ardently wanted to do right and dreaded making a mistake, but it was hard to grasp the system. In kindergarten and first grade, I couldn't tell time. I didn't know what all those bells meant or when recess was over. I misunderstood an announcement and went to an assembly on safety when I was supposed to stay in class. "Ignorance of the law is no excuse," my teacher chided me. In those early years, misunderstandings were never funny; I cried at comedies. Life was a tragedy.

Owing to some sort of casual neglect on the part of my parents, I was not baptized until I was thirteen. Fortunately, I was not alone. There were some half-dozen or so of us heathens in the communicants' class, and we were all baptized at once. Unfortunately, no one instructed us as to how, exactly, we should answer the question about our acceptance of religious responsibility.

At the critical point of our ceremonial entry into the faith, there was, accordingly, a general babble of confusion. Some said "yes," some said, "I do," one person said, "we do." That last struck me as particularly funny, the one who answered the personal conscience question on behalf of us all—a real team player. I tried not to laugh but the urge was excruciating. In a desperate attempt at subterfuge, I pretended to cough, but it came out as a ghastly burst of laughter instead. It was horrible; I couldn't stop laughing.

Granted, there was no voice from above, but this was an important perception at my semi-adult baptism. Mysteriously transported to a perspective from beyond, I suddenly saw all us participants in our common human frailty—and laughed. It was highly inappropriate behavior, yet, I dare say, a rather Christian epiphany. It was the first time I clearly recognized universal human folly, and by God, it happened in church.

Rules people, like the devoutly religious, like political zealots, like reformers or fanatics of any sort, are generally deficient in a sense of humor. This is because they have only one point of view. Irony and incongruity are not accessible to them. The notions that we are all subject to accident and forces we cannot control; that viewed from another perspective, we are all occasionally ridiculous; that there are many different dishes at the feast of life—such concepts cannot coexist with an all-consuming focus on a received code or single purpose. When there is nothing funny about not fitting in or being considered wrong, one is seldom amused.

All of this is unfortunate for it stunts imagination. And imagination, to the extent that it carries people outside of themselves and enhances tolerance, is moral. It's also a tremendous aid to learning.

Yet rules people do have the conviction of being right, and that is no mean advantage. It builds confidence and makes prompt action possible.

"Always to be right, always to trample forward, and never to doubt, are not these the great qualities with which dullness takes the lead in the world?" So asked Mr. William Makepeace Thackeray, long ago in *Vanity Fair*.

Discussion Questions

1. Review Accountability (and Responsibility). What influences our behavior besides rules and laws?
2. How does justice mean treating everyone the same? How does it mean allowing for individual differences?

Looking Back

See Attitude; Canon; Conformity; Creativity.

Looking Ahead

For discussion questions on sameness, difference, and diversity, see the questions at the end of chapter G.

E is for Effort, or Entrepreneurial, whichever works

Edge

The current prominence in business of edge and its compounds parallels its embrace of risk taking as an apparent end in itself. Through repeated linking, first, with cutting and second, with leading, business usage has given edge the properties of an attack weapon to brandish or an invasion force to lead. It has the thrill of danger without the old connotation of limit. One's learning edge, for example, is not the boundary of one's capacity but the territory one plans next to invade.

In schools, "take risks" has become a staple of commencement address imperatives, but edges in their business sense don't figure much in the verbal landscape. The concept of limitations has always been fundamental to much academic thought: art, philosophy, morality, and, most controversially, science. The edge is a line scholars are forever seeking to define. In business, it is more like a wave that cries out for a surfboard and its own keen edge.

Educate

Two philosophies are implied in the Latin origin (*educere*) of the word *educate*. "To lead forth" implies a top-down approach to teaching, teaching students what they need to know; "to draw out" implies a bottom-up approach, facilitating students' discovery of the germs of what they already know. Both have their place.

For most in the teaching profession, "to educate" represents the highest ideal of what they want to accomplish: to intensify the desire to learn, to raise the quality of, and capacity for, thought, to transcend the limitations of immediate observation and experience.

Officially, *educate* is never used in business. (See Training.) Unofficially, both businesspeople and members of the general public use it to mean "to explain the facts of life"—as in "I educated her in the realities of condominium politics." In common use, it is roughly equivalent to bringing one "up to speed."

Effective

Effective, having an effect, means getting the job done. It's an indispensable word and concept in business.

In the school world, it refers specifically to an approach to reform. The effective schools movement identifies and describes the characteristics of effective schools and implies that other schools will improve student scores by replicating those characteristics or conditions. Arthur Ellis and Jeffrey Fouts discuss the nature of the problem in chapter 7 of their work, *Research on Educational Innovations*. What it boils down to is that effective schools research has failed to show a clear connection of cause and effect.

Efficiency

Efficiency in the business sense, the maximum utilization of resources, has limited applicability in education. Schools are not efficient places. They aren't even meant to be. In America, education and child rearing are labor-intensive enterprises.

Even in the common sense of the word, schools do not much value efficiency. For example, the 80 percent/20 percent principle of time management—to wit, find the 20 percent of your work that yields 80 percent of the results and invest most of your energy into that—violates the moral emphasis in schools on effort in and of itself.

Effort

In business, one does not try; one does. The evaluation of effort in the sense of trying hard is usually reserved for situations in which the individual has less control over results but must nonetheless follow certain procedures or display specific behaviors. Thus, because it pertains to the least-powerful positions, effort is of little interest in the corporate world. "Trying hard" fits in with a slave mentality. "Nice try" is what one says to the loser.

Inasmuch as schools are supposed to teach (and measure) values as well as achievement, they create a completely different world. They deliberately build a false impression in the young that one will succeed if one tries hard and that the real world cares about effort. Many schools even symbolize the importance of effort by awarding separate grades for it. The justification for this deception is that though effort doesn't guarantee success, success in the absence of effort is also unlikely.

When students learn they've been deceived, of course, they cry out that life is unfair. Many abandon effort when they fail to achieve, finding it more honorable to be considered bad or lazy than stupid.

In the sense that teachers cannot control the native ability of their students, some consideration of teachers' efforts is also appropriate when evaluating their instructional performance. They are likely to feel as stunned as their young charges if upbraided for poor [student] performance, when they tried so hard.

Elitist

In discussions about education, "elitist" is a negative label for programs or practices that give different, presumably preferential, treatment to those with greater talent, knowledge, motivation, money, status, power, achievement records, or academic credentials than to others. It implies "unjust" and "undemocratic." When it refers to academic programs or qualifications, it also often implies "impractical."

In business, where the prevalence of the profit motive and the universal agreement on the meaning and measure of success are powerful equalizers, the word is not applicable.

Employment at Will

Textbooks say that when an employment contract falls under the heading of "employment at will," it means that either party may terminate the working relationship at any time. (See *New Encyclopedic Dictionary of Business Law—with Forms,* 2d ed.) Traditionally, most employment contracts have been oral agreements not specifying an employment period

44

of more than one year. These circumstances satisfy the general conditions for an at-will contract.

Schools come out of a different tradition. Students under the age of sixteen are compelled to attend school. This makes it difficult to fire them. Teachers usually have a one-year written contract. As with the students, then, their performance—or lack thereof—must be pretty bad to justify terminating the agreement. These are some of the legal factors favoring long-term relationships in education. There are two others to consider.

In schools, there is an institutional belief in the value of continuity, that it is better to work through the hard times—with the student, the class, the teacher—than to pull the plug on a situation, to take one's losses and write them off, as businesses can do. One reason for this is that teaching is a parenting profession. Generally, our culture disapproves of a revolving-door approach to parenting.

The other factor is that the whole teaching industry runs on a peculiar September to June school year. Industry wide, there are decision-making seasons generating tension, anxiety, and depression on a national scale followed by hiring seasons, like salmon runs. Consequences of decisions made in March, April, or May are felt any time from September through June. Teachers who wish to resign during that "year" or institutions that wish to fire face the risk of not finding suitable replacement positions or persons.

For these and other reasons, continuity, commitment, and stability—at least in appearance—tend to outweigh narrow definitions of performance or productivity.

Empowerment, Enabling

Here are two words that should be similar in meaning but are colloquial opposites.

Enable has become a doublethink word. It now commonly means not to render able, but to make less able, to lessen the capabilities of a person. It is accomplished by performing *for* a person tasks of which he or she should be capable, thereby lessening the person's confidence and ability. It is a form of intervention that impedes the learning process. Educators sometimes worry about it; progressive schools are more likely to do it than old-fashioned (strict) ones.

Empowerment, unlike *enabling*, means exactly what it says: to provide a person with additional power. Business leaders have been advocating

45

worker empowerment in lieu of middle managers, and school reformers speak variously of empowering principals, local schools, and even class-room teachers.

Despite their apparent opposition in meaning, *empowerment* and *enabling* share a common outlook. Both words imply that, left to their own devices, people have neither power, ability, nor an intrinsic desire to excel. There must be an outside power-giving or enabling source that chooses recipients from among the weak and passive. This is the histori-cal attitude toward employees, children, and teachers. It's a pessimistic view of human motivation.

Entitlement

Entitlement, as *Black's Law Dictionary* tells us, means a just and legal claim to benefits, income or property. Both employers and educators complain about an attitude of entitlement in the young. When they do, they mean a belief that one *should* get something for nothing, an attitude that im-pairs effort, performance, and productivity. Our culture and economy con-tinually reinforce the belief that "yes, you can have it all" and at little, if any, cost.

In this sense, entitlement is a kind of usurped empowerment.

Entrepreneurial

Usually followed by the word *spirit*, *entrepreneurial* represents what we like to believe is best about business and America. It suggests energy, adventurousness, initiative, originality, undaunted courage, unlimited pos-sibilities. Corporations and politicians advancing their public images make as free use of the term as songwriters did of the lyrics "fa, la, la" (to steal a joke from Henry Fielding in *Tom Jones*, book 10, chap. 2).

Like such other culture heroes as the yankee or pioneer, our Ameri-can entrepreneur is linked to an earlier, freer, simpler time in history (national or organizational), a time of fewer people and fewer regulations. People who want to improve education by making it entrepreneurial imag-ine that the pursuit of profit automatically brings freedom from constraints and a flood of innovation. There is no evidence of this.

Esteem

Building self-esteem may be in education what empowerment has been in business: a deliberate attempt by those in authority to heighten the awareness in subordinates of their own worth and potential. Though there's almost universal agreement that no one can succeed at anything without an inner sense of worth, there is much disagreement as to what brings it out.

Since having self-esteem (or feeling empowered) is positive, it is often confused with the state of feeling good. But the more one concentrates on external ways to induce a sensation of well-being in others, paternalistically providing it, the farther one strays from actually developing self-esteem.

Self-esteem ultimately is a reasonable confidence that one can master difficulty, or at least endure it intact. It's strengthened by meeting and genuinely overcoming adversity, not by avoiding it, and never by deception. A suspicion that no one expects anything from the individual tends to undermine that sense of worth. Substituting the expression "self-respect" for "self-esteem" might clarify these points.

Ethics

Ethics as an academic discipline calls for the rigorous ability to reason. It doesn't enter the high school curriculum because few in that environment are adept in abstract reasoning. On a day-to-day basis, schools tend to favor the word *values* for principles governing behavior because all but religious conservatives consider that more culturally neutral than the word *morality*. (Religious conservatives find the word *values* itself inflammatory—see "Of Human-Isms and Resources" in chap. H; Values Clarification.)

Free from such considerations, the business world is newly intoxicated with the notion of ethics. Unlike morality or integrity, which imply an internal cohesiveness based on absolute values or principles, ethics approaches behavioral choices from an abstract, analytical, and legalistic point of view. The business world loves manipulating rules.

Evaluation

Evaluation is education's word for performance appraisal or performance review, and it can apply to administrative appraisals of teachers as well as to teacher evaluations of students. Educational evaluation sounds more judgmental than performance appraisal or review because it is. It's the right name for the process.

Teachers evaluate a lot more than performance. At varying times, they assess not only students' skills, knowledge, and understanding, but their socialization (getting along, behaving oneself, being an American boy or girl) and their character (honesty, independence, effort).

Besides, for most teachers, evaluation is a tool not just for assessment, but for motivation. The educational equivalent of poetic license is called the "fudge factor." In business, that could be called favoritism or discrimination and end in lawsuit.

Excellence

Excellence has had a great run of popularity in business, but is being edged out by the less-absolute word, *quality.*

Most Americans don't really like the idea of excellence because it is undemocratic. Most want to be just slightly above average, and that is what they want for their children. The ideal is to be pretty good at a number of things but not stand out at anything in particular.

The one place where excellence still is considered acceptable is in school. "Brains" and honor-roll students may have to endure teasing and verbal abuse, but getting an "excellent" on a test, paper, or lab report is still considered a good thing. This may be something positive for schools and business to build on.

Experiential Learning

Experiential learning is a fancy term for the School of Hard Knocks: what you learned as a result of having done something. "Hands-on learning" and "learning by doing" are similar expressions.

Business leaders are very keen on the concept of experiential learning in the schools. For those who are impatient with theory themselves, it is easy to dismiss the academic emphasis on theory as yet another indication of befuddlement and incompetence. Besides, adults tend to favor this form of learning.

In and of itself, hands-on learning isn't adequate for achieving workforce readiness, not if that means able to learn, as the prophets keep telling us. Monkey see, monkey do is effective for meeting performance goals, yet not the same as monkey think. Monkey need some abstract learning as well, and monkey won't figure it out alone.

48

◆ ◆ ◆

Of Teacher Evaluation
and Teachers' Evaluations

The ambiguity of the term "teacher evaluation" is rich in significance. A teacher-evaluation form can mean either a form on which teachers evaluate students or a form on which students or administrators evaluate teachers. The interdependency of the performance issue creates a more fluid evaluation process than any one finds in business as usual. Some would say it's more confused.

When students (or parents) behave like customers, they freely evaluate teachers. And like customers, they are listened to. Usually, the situation is one in which no news is good news. Many a teacher, justly or unjustly, has been drummed out of employment by a vociferous campaign of students and parents. Sincere, hard-working teachers sometimes resent the factors that can make colleagues popular. It's tempting to think that Iago's statement that reputation is oft got without merit and lost without deserving was custom-designed by Shakespeare as former schoolmaster.

When students are considered workers, teachers become their supervisors, managers, and mentors; they coach, motivate, and evaluate their workers/students. In business, the role of manager as teacher is a relatively new concept still being enthusiastically introduced; in education, that combination of roles is old.

When students are viewed as products, various attempts are made to assess their quality. In this way, people hope to determine the effectiveness of the individuals and institutions that produced them. Besides, since no one has proposed a way to measure the influence of, say, peers, parents, community, and media on student performance, systems designed to measure student performance tend to place the entire responsibility for learning on the teacher.

As performance measurements, test scores probably have greatest appeal within the business community and those influenced by it because they yield numbers and can be graphed. This preference remains despite such well-known criticisms of standardized testing as

1. *Lack of national or local consensus as to what should be tested and how*

49

2. *Cultural bias in tests*
3. *Tendency of tests to be designed for ease of scoring rather than the optimum evaluation of knowledge or skill tested*
4. *Directing teaching toward success on tests of questionable value*
5. *Adverse impact on curriculum (possible built-in bias toward objective, measurable content)*
6. *Cheating—by students and/or teachers*
7. *Implied unrealistic expectation of continuous improvement (growth occurs in spurts, not quarters)*
8. *Uncertainty as to basis of test score comparisons*

Why— besides clarity and simplicity—do test scores remain the most popular measure among the public? Consider the alternative: grades.

To a cynical observer, it would appear unlikely that teacher evaluations of students could have any validity whatsoever—not if they're used to show teacher effectiveness. Should not our circumstances resemble those in the Stalinist USSR, in which the success of teachers was judged by the success of their students, with the result that pupils were unlikely to get a failing grade? And are not teachers, who can make themselves look good by making their students look good, in a situation almost as luxurious as the one for which CEOs have been so criticized: in effect, of hiring their own bosses by selecting the board of directors that assesses their performance and sets their compensation?

To make matters still worse, it would be hard to find a teacher who seriously maintained that his or her grades were a truly precise, objective measurement. Most would freely admit that they are designed (almost) as much to motivate (manipulate) as to measure. "So-and-so needed a boost; so-and-so needed to be shaken up." As tools, grades are as often jacks or hammers as they are yardsticks. And when it comes to grading, all teachers, departments, and schools need to make some accommodation on the various aspects of their mission to young people. Somehow achievement, aptitude, and societal values all need to be taken into account.

It used to be, for example, that students who didn't perform well were told to "try harder," an injunction that gained notoriety once learning disabilities were discovered. In fact, it became very difficult to suggest that anyone "try harder" without being suspected of insensitivity. On the other hand, there is also the mission of schools to support the work ethic, to resist an attitude of entitlement, to advance self-discipline and performance whether they yield a reward or just give the student practice in

50

stoical endurance when life is hard. In this connection, "try harder" is perfectly legitimate, even valuable advice.

Yet what does experience teach us about teacher evaluations in the face of all these variations? Surprisingly, colleges say that high school grades are the best single predictors of academic success. Parents commonly express amazement at how well and how quickly teachers come to know their children. And generally speaking, even radically different teachers, with radically different approaches, philosophies, and styles, come to similar conclusions about the same kids. Why? Who knows. Maybe it has to do with being professional, or having the gift.

Do school grades have anything to do with job or life performance? We don't know. That's because the general public considers teacher evaluations important only as long as students are locked inside the closed academic system. Afterward, grades are forgotten or ignored. Only recently have some groups actually proposed considering grades as a factor in hiring. Perhaps more should look into these questions.

Discussion Questions

1. Consider the qualities that make a good person, a good learner, a good worker, and a good businessperson. How are they compatible? How do they conflict?
2. What do your conclusions suggest about teaching and evaluating students?
3. What do they suggest about evaluating teachers?
4. List and discuss "E" words suggesting that educational institutions are purveyors of values that are not esteemed in the world of business.

For Further Consideration

1. What roles do, or should, effort, respect, and self-esteem play in worker empowerment?
2. What can managers and teachers learn from each other about what to do and what not to do?

Looking Ahead

See Fair, Fairness; Flexibility.

F is for Flexible

Facts

Except in the higher reaches of academe, our cultural faith in the fact is universal. Our main requirements of facts are that they be substantives (unemployment; aluminum; President Hoover), numbers (50 percent; nine big ones), or assertions (hot air rises; possession is nine-tenths of the law). They appeal to our moral and aesthetic bias toward simplicity and are thus broadly equated with truth.

Facts need not be linked in any meaningful or coherent way to be persuasive; indeed, even irrelevant facts seem hard to refute. In business and politics, where they are rhetorical tools dissociated from learning, inquiry, or the pursuit of truth, they are constantly invoked. Business and political leaders are highly skilled in the effective use of facts.

When they consider school reform, however, businesspeople tend to favor instruction in thinking skills over a command of "mere facts." Here they might be mirroring the ambivalence of educators themselves, who have vacillated for decades between the virtues of content, on one hypothetical hand, and skills on another.

Failure

No one likes this word. The least objectionable use occurs in connection with technology—as in "There was a system failure." Such an expression takes on the cast of an act of God.

Business failures usually go by better names. To be "in Chapter 11," for example, is often like a mere developmental phase. Students prefer to admit they flunked, which is more like striking out, a single act rather than the generalized condition implied in the word *failure.*

Failure usually raises the question of fault, as in "Why did you fail me?" or "I didn't fail you; you failed yourself."

Fair, Fairness

Fairness is an old issue in schools and a new one in business. While it takes considerable maturity to embrace the abstract notion of justice, most people suffer—early, immediately, and personally—from violations of fairness: at home, on the playground, in the classroom. Those who move on to attain power usually cease to concern themselves with it (unless, of course, they also happen to become interested in justice). It remains an issue chiefly among the powerless.

Teachers, then, who work with children and generally lack positional power, are forever defining, negotiating, redefining, defending, and upholding fairness. The profession is steeped in the language of accommodation: headstart, second chance, time out, extra credit, retake, rematch, bending over backwards, grading on a curve, rounded up, averaged out, thrown in for good measure, more or less. The appearance of precision is constantly undermined by the fairness yardstick.

In business, policy and legislation have traditionally controlled these areas; as long as one demonstrated compliance, there was no need for personal judgment. But rules, or at least styles, appear to be changing. More and more, managers are urged to be flexible and fair as work patterns and worker populations change. Like it or not, more and more managers are in the role of school teacher, making judgment calls and defending them as individuals instead of purveyors of policy. Perhaps they could learn something from teachers.

Faster

In education, *faster* is an accepted euphemism for *smarter*. In business, faster also means better. (See Speed.)

The world has always heaped early rewards on what used to be called "fast wits," though they often outlive their glory. The question of who wins the race has a lot to do with the length of the course.

Feedback

Before the field of electronics brought us the word *feedback*, we used such words as *response, reaction, opinion, evaluation, judgment, critique, criticism, feeling,* and so on. The mechanistic neutrality of the term makes any such judgment seem less personally threatening and more objective.

References to feedback are equally prevalent in the brother-sister social sciences of business and education, and the actual application equally rare. Opportunities abound to master the art of giving and receiving feedback, but the widespread dread of doing either remains a block to authentic learning in the workplace as well as academe. (See Input.)

Flat

Flat in education or the arts usually means boring, uninteresting. In business, it refers to organizations that have shed unnecessary layers (often middle managers). The idea is to create an organization that is more participative, egalitarian, fast, responsive—and less costly. *Flat*, then, may here also retain some of its colloquial sense of bankrupt or broke.

Flexibility

Teachers are so much in the habit of valuing flexibility, they have little need to advocate it among themselves.

Business, with its tradition of fidelity to a single purpose, its visions, missions, goals, targets, objectives, strategic planning, and its inspired linear mindset generally, is quite different. There, to change one's mind or to deviate from course is to lose.

Flexibility in benefits, work arrangements, compensation plans, performance review systems, and even management styles does not come naturally to this world, however enlightened its practitioners seem. The fundamental reason corporate change is hard is that it implies one was

54

once mistaken. It is hard to overcome the feeling that it indicates weakness.

Nevertheless, business organizations that have been flattened require greater flexibility among the survivors. It's a highly desirable quality in the overworked, as any boarding-school teacher knows.

Free Enterprise

Textbooks agree that the economic system of free enterprise is rooted in private ownership and individual initiative, motivated by the desire to make a profit. In free enterprise, there is an absence of central economic control. Instead, the many independent, individual decisions made by producers and consumers are kept in a sort of order by competitive pricing and the interflow of supply and demand. People who are used to the system admire its freedom and flexibility; those unaccustomed to it consider it chaotic (*McGraw-Hill Dictionary of Modern Economics,* 3d ed.).

Education is a public as well as a private concern. It acknowledges, relies on, and often even encourages motives other than a desire for profit as inducement to initiative. One of its purposes is to inform education consumers as to what they need to consume. This calls at least for some modification in the operation of supply and demand.

Does it make sense to use one economic system as a total philosophy of life?

✦ ✦ ✦

ABCs for Business
and Academe Reconsidered

Sometimes I wonder if businesspeople ever see in schools a warning of what could be menacing them. American education has, after all, been charged with carrying more and more of our national social mission. It's had to replace the church and family. Education has had to deal with ethnic diversity long before that became something to crow about. It was expected (with minimal funding) to wage war against drugs, venereal disease, television, and the neglect of children. In the early 1980s, it had to make everybody instantly computer literate, all ages at once (including teachers), across the board—no wonder the First and Second Punic Wars—and cultural literacy—were jettisoned.

And where has the torch of our national social mission been passing?

To business, of course. "Don't trust government. Give the problems to business. They know how to get things done—and they have the pockets to fund it." From the business point of view, such flattery has its cost. Some might worry that the school bell could be tolling for business, too.

If we permit ourselves to consider the failures, have not American schools and business been opposite sides of the same coin? Both flourished in another time. But many businesses failed to keep up with late twentieth-century change, while schools tried to respond to all of it, charged with carrying the social agenda everyone else was dropping from lack of funds, energy, or will. Toward the seeming end of the American era, business has been told to get sensitive; schools, to get tough.

In some ways, the businesses that are surviving have shown more capacity to learn than the schools have. Progressive schools could learn from them about planning and sticking to a plan; they could learn that feeling good doesn't have to mean an extended vacation from reality. Traditional schools could learn that business has stopped segmenting work into specialized jobs and has started saying it values thought and creativity, not just conformity.

At the same time, business has a lot to gain from the schools. Many of the forces that hit schools in the 1960s and 1970s have hit business in the 1980s and 1990s, where they've been handled, if not by better problem solvers, at least by better publicists. Those that want to learn more about treating people humanely, appreciating differences, and bringing out variant forms of *best* would do well to study what's worked and not worked in the schools. The new business and the new education could very well reinforce in each other the ideas that showing up isn't enough, that performance counts, that human beings have many ways to contribute—and may even enjoy doing so.

Does all this mean that the interests of the two institutions should merge, that American education should quite literally mean the same things as business? Personally, I'm not prepared to say so. Whatever it may say in its more grandiose moments, business does not exist to inquire into meaning but to make money. The world it promises is too small a piece of the whole. And whatever it may say in its missionary zeal about shaping up the young, business has itself beamed out a constant message to our future workforce that life is meant for the continuous consumption of pleasures. Children have high, though false, hopes clearly implanted in them long before they even enter the schoolhouse. Some of them impede learning.

If we think in terms of national balance, we can ask what other secular institution we have to support the pursuit of truth, the impractical, the imaginative, and purely idealistic that we need to sustain our culture, if not academe. Where else do we produce those who ultimately prod and shame the darker side of business? At the same time, to the extent that, for generations, our most elite schools have perpetuated the worship of money and power and our public schools have been conceived as assembly lines producing the ideal nineteenth-century laborer, they have fallen short of their educational ideals.

Surely workforce readiness is one of many other excellent motives for the enhancement of learning.

Questions to Reconsider

1. To what extent does business seem to be adapting attitudes characteristic of education and education of business?
2. How could such a switch be explained?
3. What roles do, or should, effort, respect, and self-esteem play in worker empowerment?
4. What can managers and teachers learn from each other about what to do and what not to do?
5. How do issues of fairness and flexibility fit into the present worlds of business and education?
6. Does it make sense to use one economic system as a total philosophy of life?

G means Groups and Goals

Gainsharing

While society gains when everybody learns or performs, our reward and motivation systems are geared toward the individual who gains at the expense of others. Gainsharing is a newer form of compensation in the business world that provides a group reward for group performance. Key to its success are involvement of employees in setting a common goal with measurable results. In schools, cooperative education uses similar methods to spread the reward of group learning.

Businesses are still deciding by experiment if and whether such a system can be integrated with systems, like merit pay, that reward individual performance. Classroom teachers often consider when to encourage competition among individuals and when to encourage sharing. Schools not only serve society collectively, they socialize individuals. Sometimes these interests conflict. (See Team Performance [Evaluation and Reward].)

Gender

Gender should be a neutral term. In reality, it almost always refers to females as the group most recently added to the human species in the human consciousness. In this respect, it is similar to the noun *co-ed*, which, though it abbreviates "coeducational student," refers only to women who joined in belatedly on universal education.

Gender studies are often conducted in academe. Workshops or training sessions on gender issues also occur in businesses adjusting to a larger female presence. Gender studies usually emphasize gender differences in a nonjudgmental fashion; thus they tend to favor females. (For specific issues, see Women in Business; Women in Education.)

Generalization

This is the common term for what philosophers and educators call induction—that is, coming to general conclusions from observation of, and experience with, individual occurrences. Up through high school, students are encouraged to generalize. It's part of teaching people to think on an abstract level. Early on in college, however, students are cautioned against generalizing prematurely or recklessly. The attitudes that adults in ordinary life have about generalizations often reflect how much education they have had or where their intellectual development has stopped.

Stereotypes are one sort of irresponsible generalization that causes difficulty—especially among those concerned with managing diversity.

Gifted

Gifted is the term in education for people with potential for doing extraordinarily well in one or more areas.

A gift is something one got for nothing. The term is not used in business. There, promising employees are said to have potential and are unabashedly dubbed "fast track." The attitude is not considered elitist, but rather, competitive. If they fail to perform, they're deemed bad hires who didn't come through. No one asks if they were bored.

Glass Ceiling

This refers to the unofficial barrier to professional advancement that people outside the power structure (women and minorities) encounter in business. The metaphor suggests that one looks up to a great height to which one aspires but is actually held down by invisible obstacles, some of which may be unrecognized vestiges of the old system. Concern about the glass ceiling represents a second phase of expanding opportunities. The feeling is that while many of the previously excluded are now getting hired, they still do not have equivalent upward mobility.

Though the term hasn't been applied to the educational system, it fits this great embodiment of our national culture. All have been welcomed—indeed, compelled—into the system, and in many ways, it has been a great equalizer, opening opportunity to our constant stream of newcomers. Yet at the same time, early sorting procedures build in the ceilings that affect later ascent in life. Our next phase may be figuring out how to give to those that have *and* to those that have not.

Global

Businesses that crossed national boundaries used to be called international or multinational. Global, referring to the entire world, gained popularity in the expansionist 1980s. It has a special connotation of power and empire.

In education, *global*, meaning whole and holistic, has been around longer. Global education has been a popular type of integrated, multidisciplinary study. Robin Barrow and Geoffrey Milburn discuss it in their entries on "Integrated studies" and "Topic-centred education" (*A Critical Dictionary of Educational Concepts,* 2d ed.). Generally, educators understand global IQ to mean one's total score reflecting overall mental ability (*Dictionary of Education*). Specifically, though, a "global" intelligence is one that intuits, integrates, and generalizes. (See, for example, Arthur Ellis and Jeffrey Fouts, *Research on Educational Innovations*, pp. 65, 67, and 191.)

In both arenas, *global* refers to an ability to think broadly. In business, it suggests a breadth and boldness that find opportunity and conquest anywhere. In education, it's sometimes an indirect way of suggesting carelessness about detail.

Goal

Purpose words (go*al, objective, target, mission, vision, philosophy, road map*) seem to have enjoyed a special burst of popularity at the same time that complaints about leadership voids (in politics, business, education, general earth management) have swelled. It could be that when people no longer respond to injunctions like "trust me," they want to see the printed route or recipe for themselves. Or it could be that the late-twentieth-

60

century flourishing of purpose words is our chosen way of ending the era that created the existential Void and the worship of spontaneity.

Much labor has gone into distinguishing various purpose words in print. In both business and education, the most commonly paired and distinguished words are *goals* and *objectives*. The goal is the desired end result; objectives (usually plural) are smaller ends or purposes that, collectively, serve as means to the ultimate goal. The goal is long-term and the objective(s) closer to hand. To use the favorite metaphor: the goal is to win the game; the objectives are to keep the ball in play, to stay within the lines, to prevent the opponent from scoring, to avoid incurring penalties, and to score as many points as possible.

The new emphasis on goals and objectives perhaps represents the triumph of linear thinking in our culture. It is better than not thinking at all, even though it is well documented that much valuable learning and creative thinking occur mysteriously off the subject.

Grade School, Grammar School

We seem to have trouble deciding whether to designate our schools by what is taught in them or by when they come in a sequence.

"Grammar school," the most old-fashioned name for elementary school, refers ultimately to the content taught. Since ancient times, our culture has considered language—including rhetoric, logic, and grammar—the core of an education. (For real-life significance, see Participation; Politics; Prep, Private [and Independent] School.)

The name "grade school" shows a shift from content to process. It refers to a school in which students are segregated by age and placed in grades in linear succession. This is the industrial-age image of the school.

The terms *elementary* (grades K-6) and *primary* (grades K-3) are both ambiguous. They refer to what comes first, either in content/skill importance—the basics—or merely in chronological sequence—the start.

Grass Roots

This is the sociopolitical term for democratic, bottom-to-top initiatives. Grass-roots movements have more obvious, immediate impact on the parts of the educational system that are community-based than they can have on business.

In business, grass-roots movements are detected by market research. Within companies, they are structured as suggestion systems, employee involvement programs, team-building initiatives, and the like. Even business leaders bred under the strong-arm tactics of yore are likely to talk favorably of grass-roots movements—unless, of course, the grass fails to bend to their wishes. Grass roots, in the form of employees, can still be turned to scorched earth.

Group

Business structures, by their very nature, are highly concerned with designating and organizing groups of people. Businesses, indeed, have so many specific designations for groups, such as, departments, divisions, units, associates, organizations, companies, teams, task forces, corporations, they perhaps don't need this schoolroom word. One exception was a fashion in the 1960s to name companies "groups": The Something Group, rather than Something Associates. The term still has an unmistakable elegance about it that is almost elitist.

Group is an important word in psychology, sociology, and education. Teachers are always concerned with group dynamics and often devise group activities and projects to foster learning.

"Stay with the group" is an elemental field-trip order, the primordial key to survival.

Guru

The rise to prominence of the word *guru* shows both the appeal in business of new-age thinking and some slowness to internalize it. Business gurus generally espouse such advanced ideas as participative management. Yet the very prevalence and veneration of the *guru* in the corporate world suggests its deep-rooted addiction to authority. There is a kind of instinct to learn from what the gifted man preaches from on high.

Teachers by nature and tradition are more quarrelsome and disrespectful of any authority other than their own. Mostly, they don't like gurus.

✦ ✦ ✦

In Search of Charles Redman

All through the years of the Reagan administration, I was consumed with one question: Was the State Department's official spokesperson, Charles

62

Redman, the boy I went to sixth grade with at Edgewood Junior High School?

There was more to my drive to know the truth than "auld lang syne." In part, I was looking for proof that some careers, at least in retrospect, are predictable, that there are people in the world who follow an immutable trajectory from the earliest phases of life.

My Charles Redman (and he was always Charles, by the way, never Charlie or Chuck) was exceptionally interested in, and precociously well-informed about, politics and current events. In fact, he and another boy, Brian Mark, entirely shaped the whole sixth grade experience.

Sixth grade, I should explain, was the first year of our regional junior high school, so all of us pubescent children were subjected to the additional trauma of confronting a room of strangers in September. Yet the merger of Charles and Brian was like the convergence of two hemispheres, a whole new world that dazzled us with its brilliance. They shared the passion for politics, but Charles was a Republican and Brian was a Democrat. They instantly became best friends and sparring partners as was meant to be.

Charles and Brian dominated the whole year. Sometimes together and sometimes separately, they presented an incredible variety of homemade quiz and game shows, always on politics and current events. Even at this distance in time, I can't imagine how the humorless, colorless, dandruff-riddled Miss Patterson felt about these strange boys who considered learning fun and ran away with her class and time-honored lesson plans. Each youngster was poised, well-dressed, and articulate, standing before a map, screen, or chalkboard, pointer in hand. How could Charles have become anything *but* a spokesperson for the State Department? He even had a kingly name.

For years, then, I tortured myself wondering if these two Charles Redmans were identical. But as the second term of the Reagan administration drew toward its close, I realized I had to act before I lost the chance to reach him. This posed a whole new set of dilemmas.

Once I acquired the State Department's address, I began to wonder who would open the letter. I worried it would be an officious underling who'd think I was a kook, some latter-day Carol Burnett, in love with some latter-day John Foster Dulles. I was afraid if I wrote "personal" on the envelope, it would immediately be forwarded to the FBI, CIA, and IRS, and my taxes would be audited for the next forty years. "I'm only a woman," I'd have to say somewhere. "We're supposed to be the gender that cares about sustaining relationships."

Then, even if he *was* the right Charles Redman, how would I make him see the cosmic importance of his identity? How would I make him understand the question was really related to my quest for the meaning of life?

To prepare for the possibility that he wasn't the right Charles Redman, I decided to include a self-addressed, stamped postcard on which he could check the appropriate response. That would indicate my respect for him as a busy employee of the State Department.

My next problem was how to let him know who *I* was. I was chagrined to find that I seemed to remember everybody else in the class better than I did myself. There was the class behavior problem, Joel Brash (who says one's name doesn't affect one's character?). There was the smart, plump, unhappy Janet Barnard who was the first girl I knew to go through that peculiar compulsion to change names that afflicts many young teens ("Jan," "Janette," "Jeannie"). There was Hollydale Shapiro, with the long red pony tail and the long skinny legs, who suffered the humiliation of being told by Miss Patterson that her Halloween costume (a ballerina tutu) was indecent and she should change back into her school clothes at once.

But who was I? I wasn't on a career trajectory like Charles, and thanks to my habit of always being absent on class photo day, I couldn't even send him a picture. I could remind him I was a finalist in one of Brian's geography games, until I missed the Bay of Bengal, but that might have slipped his mind.

I considered opening with something snappy like, "You perhaps remember my witty report on Saskatchewan," but dismissed it as another dead end. All the exciting provinces—Quebec, Nova Scotia, British Columbia—got picked off right away, so I picked a province no one else in the class would want. Original, yes, but hard to convert into an interesting report. My device was to make a puppet of Saskatchewan and present it as an interview with the province itself. Of course, Saskatchewan also lacks an interesting shape, and my interview was with a kind of talking trapezoid that really didn't have much to say for itself.

Finally, how could I let Charles Redman know that another of Miss Patterson's students came to a not unworthy end, however modest and unexpected?

Considering these difficulties was enough to discourage me from even asking. But Charles Redman was my test case, and I steeled myself for it.

G   G means Groups and Goals

Did something in life really happen as it was meant to? I *had* to know the truth, deciding that if I did and if he *was* my Charles Redman, I'd be left with only one more imponderable. What ever happened to Brian Mark?

Discussion Questions

1. Does the importance of group values (being like others) conflict with the importance of individual values (being unique, different from others) in theory? In practice?
2. Where should the emphasis be placed—on group or individual values—in a learning environment? In a work environment? In society?
3. How does justice mean treating everyone the same? How does it mean allowing for individual differences?
4. What is gained when pursuing clearly defined goals and objectives? What is lost?

Looking Back

Review Career.

Looking Ahead

To continue the discussion of sameness and difference, see chapter N and the closing questions.

H is for Human(e?) Resources

Hands-On

Hands-on learning is learning by doing. It is probably the preferred learning style of most adults who have lost patience with (or despaired of grasping) the theoretical approach and want results.

When applied to simulated experiences, hands-on is always favorable. A very hands-on approach purports to be exciting, immediate, and authentic.

In management, hands-on is bad. A hands-on manager fails to delegate as he or she should and is both personally inefficient and demotivating to others. *Micromanagement* is a pejorative synonym. Teachers with this style are called enablers. In environments that approve of such a style, they are called supportive.

Hierarchy in Business

The hierarchy as a principle of organization is based on the belief that not all persons, ideas, or things are equal and that there is a series of gradations from least to most, worst to best, and so forth.

Hierarchies have been overthrown and decreed dead many times throughout history. Sometimes politics or ideas upset them and sometimes technology does (e.g., gunpowder, mass production, microchips). As Americans, our theoretical democratic convictions resist hierarchies; our practical requirements and habits of mind depend upon them.

In the present business climate, the hierarchy is (once again) under a death sentence. The old-fashioned, top-down, military-church hierarchy is derided as hopelessly unenlightened and doomed to extinction. The authority for these views comes straight from the top; our leaders explain their insights thus:

"To remain competitive* and respond to the rapid change* in today's global* environment, organizations must restructure* and become leaner,* meaner,* and flatter* (cutting the fat from the middle). They must create a new culture,* in which performance-* and quality-* driven* teams* are empowered* and trained* in the problem-solving* skills* needed for productive* bottom-up decision making.* Top management* no longer 'manages'*; it 'leads.'*" (*See appropriate entries.)

We might note in passing that the hierarchical head of business still remains and that the most odious features of the hierarchy are thought to reside in those organizational tiers that have included king-deposing barons, pope-poisoning cardinals, coup d'état-designing generals, and savvy middle managers.

Hierarchy in Education

The current mood to repudiate hierarchy (and bureaucracy) is as strong in education as in business, though the issues, whether organizational decision making, redistribution of power, curriculum content, or preferred teaching style, are more highly contested. Perhaps this is because the earliest and most familiar model of the hierarchy is the family, in which

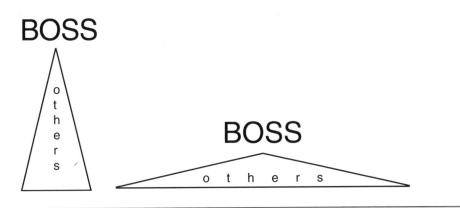

H is for Human(e?) Resources   **H**

the younger are answerable to the older, the smaller to the larger, the weaker to the stronger, the inexperienced to the seasoned.

The family analogy is powerful in schools, which consist—literally—of older, more knowledgeable, and experienced people teaching younger, greener ones. The questions then become who parents the next generation in a democracy and, most broadly, who are the adults and who are the children? More pragmatic questions are these:

- *Should public education be more centralized (with state or national standards) or more locally controlled (by parents and community standards)?*
- *Are some things more important to learn than others?*
- *Are some people better equipped by virtue of their knowledge, training, judgment, and experience to make these decisions than others?*
- *Are schools in part conveyors of a common cultural heritage, or are they only to propagate right thinking as presently or locally understood?*
- *Does taking a vote or survey yield the best result or merely the least-divisive one? Must the result be best?*

History

American culture has always been more oriented toward the present and future than the past. We are the land of fresh-starters. Business, too, has tended to view "past history" as something to surpass (the lower left-hand corner of the graph). "It's history" is a commonly accepted way of saying, "It's *finito*; down the tubes."

To the extent that institutions of learning have been charged with remembering and transmitting the past, they have often been dismissed as irrelevant. Some recent educators have perhaps made amends by eliminating anything that can be classified as memory-based from the learning experience.

Yet despite such deep distrust, the past has drawn more favorable press as awareness of corporate culture spreads. One possibly inconvenient result of corporate restructuring is that fewer and fewer people remain in organizations who can even remember how they got where they are.

Holistic

Holistic has a new-age aura and is therefore inflammatory in certain circles. Educators have tried to elude attacks from religious conservatives by spelling the word correctly (see, for example, Whole Child; Whole Language), but this evasive maneuver has not always succeeded.

The appeal of the word seems to spring from a desire in our fragmented society for wholeness. Despite its traditional preference for specialization and narrowness of focus, even business is making greater use of the term and concept as it advocates sharing the vision, cross training among team members, and a seamless organization designed only to serve the customer.

For some reason, religious conservatives don't attack business interests.

Human Asset Accounting, Human Capital

Whether human beings feel demeaned or exalted when considered a form of material goods probably varies with their definitions of worth. The business world coined the expressions "human asset" and "human capital" and, in its upper echelons, obviously considers them a gracious way of bestowing and recognizing value. (Cf. Human Resources.)

We speak of investing in our children and in our future. We still don't refer to children as our capital. There might be some who would find the term offensive.

Humane, Humanist, Humanistic, Humanize, Humanism

The adjectives *humane* and *humanistic*, the noun *humanist*, and the verb *humanize* appear from time to time in the business world. Generally, they are used to note something other than business as usual. A humane company, for example, is one that is distinguished by its care for human beings as people within or beyond its boundaries.

Educators see attention to students (human beings) as fundamental to their business. It appears unnecessary to name things that are taken for granted.

In higher education, the words *humane, humanist,* and *humanistic* (also *humanism* and *humanities*) have special meanings rooted in our Western cultural heritage and therefore do not concern most people. *Humanize*

69

still means to endow with human qualities, but is applied only to nonhuman entities such as animals, machines, or other inanimate objects. Academic purists would consider it tautological to speak of humanizing something human. Only business has the need to point out periodically that humans may be human.

Of Human-Isms and Resources

Historically, business has divided its operations between the business side, taken care of by line, and the people side, taken care of by staff. Following the military model, those who focused on people (personnel) were not in the chain of command since they didn't work toward the primary mission of the business: to capture wealth. They merely provided support.

This is the historical chip human resource (HR) professionals carry on their shoulders, and the human words in business should probably be understood in this context. Proclamations about the importance of people ("Our employees are our greatest asset") are spoken with the zeal of the recently converted and figure in a campaign that is still under way. No longer, says the campaign, are people cannon fodder. No longer is there the split between staff and line.

On the other hand, the human words stand in a long and revered tradition in Western learning, representing the pinnacles of Western achievement: our basic system of rational thought, our standards of scholarly accuracy, our efforts to pursue a good, virtuous, and fulfilling life with, or without, divine inspiration and sanctions. For most (but naturally not all) scholars, humanistic movements represent a return to one of the basic sources of our culture.

As an intellectual movement associated with the Renaissance revival of ancient learning, for example, humanism was either secular or Christian. (Included in the Christian strand were such notables as Erasmus of Rotterdam, Saint Thomas More, and John Milton of *Paradise Lost* fame.) Both strands stressed the importance of human learning and reason as a means to goodness, as did Enlightenment thinking in the eighteenth century. It seems that whenever we need a you-can-do-it message in our culture, some form of humanism appears to save us from deterministic despair. And whenever we get too self-indulgent, too puffed up and full of ourselves, we have an outburst of fundamentalism to remind us we're no good—or at least, not as good or self-sufficient as we think we are.

70

If two men could produce a child, the parents of our nation might be Jonathan Edwards and Thomas Jefferson. And if we speak spiritually, not chronologically, their child would have been the hybrid Ben Franklin, from whom we are all descended. American education has often served the practical and materialistic interests of our father's business, but it has also been the institution that's sustained the eighteenth-century idealism still in our spiritual genes (or *memes*, to use the new word).

Leaving these nuances aside, rank-and-file religious conservatives tend to equate all forms of humanism with secular humanism, considering no threat more monstrous. They see the public school system as dangerously under its influence. If they know there are distinctions between Christian humanism, Renaissance secular humanism, and the twentieth-century psychological theory of behavior also called humanism, they don't care. At root, they see all as a denial of original sin and divinely sanctioned absolutes. Religious conservatives have the classic theory X worldview that says, among other things, if you don't lock the fire doors, the workers will steal the chickens. (See Theories X and Y, chap. XYZ.)

By rights, or the laws of rational consistency, these conservatives should object as passionately to the attempted cultural changes in corporate America, empowering the worker, as they do to remnants of humanism in education. In fairness, though, such refined distinctions are rather hard to make. The puritan strand in our culture has taught us that the generation of wealth is a sign of divine Grace. Business, then, *must* be good, and schools should mind the store—that is, teach their charges those necessary practical skills required to go forth and gather wealth.

Human Resources

In business, the preferred term for what they call the people side of the business is human resources (HR) and human resource management. The earlier term *personnel* is now pretty much in disgrace, implying a petty, literal-minded focus on rules, formalism, procedures, forms, policies, paper, and bureaucratic obstacles. The myopic personnel mentality fragments in order to cope. It "doesn't get it." HR has a far nobler purpose.

Human resource management synthesizes and integrates; it is visionary. It implies the enlightened view of employees as the company's greatest asset, inextricably linked, after all, to the business side of the business, which is the bottom line. All is one.

71

As a term, human resources could be considered inspiration, paradox, sophistry, metaphor, doublethink, or reverse psychology. It affirms the importance of people, not because they are people, but because they *aren't* people; properly considered, it claims, people are just as valuable as any other resource. To appreciate the subtlety of the message, you might imagine Jesus saying, "Love your neighbor as your camel or your water rights."

So-called business offices in educational institutions, regardless of the humanity of the learning environment itself, are still largely run along the old, personnel-office model. The mission, then, of the educator's personnel or business office is to say nay and cite the correct reason for doing so.

Humor

The business world is not noted for its sense of humor. To be sure, formal jokes, with clear conventions of their own, are certainly allowed, and skill in delivering them is a distinct social and professional asset. Periodically, too, experts write books or offer workshops on how to use or interject humor into certain situations. Their advice, however, is steeped in caution.

Why is business so generally humorless? First, humor is not a thing to be interjected, but a way to view the world. In fact, it requires multiple ways to view the world, as in irony and incongruity. These are not accessible to those who have a single focus, such as the bottom line or other espoused mission.

Second, the essential notions for humor, that we are all subject to accident and forces we cannot control, are anathema to the can-do world of business. Humor may very well be the best way there is of expressing doubt, confusion, and humility, but these are not winning qualities.

To the extent that educators regard themselves as sublime authorities or model themselves on businesspeople, they also are humorless. To the extent that they genuinely observe and think, find people and language of interest, are unpretentious and intellectually honest, they have great senses of humor. This causes people to think they aren't serious. Why can't they get down to business?

Humor, by the way, was originally a moisture or fluid. The opposite of *humorous* is not *serious*; it's *dry* or *rigid.*

Looking Ahead

To pursue a discussion of fragmentation and integration, parts and wholes, see the questions at the end of chapter K. For further consideration of the issue of human worth, see chapters V and W.

I equals Integrity

Idealist

Technically, an idealist is one who believes in the ultimate reality of ideas and mental activity. The mind makes the world.

Commonly, to be idealistic means to be unrealistic, and often, naive. Our culture doesn't believe in ideas; we believe in sense, or information that comes through our senses. To most people, idealism also suggests a faith in goodness that hasn't yet run aground on the rocks of experience.

Academics often use philosophical terms in their original, more restricted senses. This makes them misunderstood and thought to speak nonsense. Businesspeople speak more like everybody else.

Identity

Identity and *identical* both come from the Latin word for the same. A person with a strong identity is s*emper idem*, always the same. Establishing one's identity is a principal task in marking the passage from childhood to adulthood.

In business, adults speak not of identity, but of career plateauing, stagnation, passages, or midlife crises. An enormous industry exists to advise people in how to assume the identity of a new position and play the required part. (See Role.) Unsuccessful job applicants are often told they are not a match or a fit. That means they do not appear identical with the part they are to play.

Of course, we teach the young very early that their identity comes from what they do for a living when we ask them, "What do you want to be when you grow up?" The question as to which comes first, the job or the identity, may be moot.

Imagination (and Innovation)

Imagination is a mysterious ability to synthesize, often by leaps over unseen connectors. Great lip service is paid to it in elementary school, though it receives less time, praise, and attention as the school years advance. Sometimes when teachers tell parents their child has a great imagination, they are euphemistically suggesting the child lies.

Business focuses on the end result of imagination and calls it innovation. Innovation is valuable because it provides an edge or leg up on the competition. Though it would be logical to value imagination as the precursor of innovation, imagination doesn't necessarily yield results, in which case, it merely wastes time, hurts productivity, and establishes its possessor as a bad organizational match.

Incentive

In both business and education, an incentive is a promised reward designed to spur desired action. It's an external motivator that is nearly always monetary in business. Business-oriented groups try to help schools by offering to fund other incentives (discounts, T-shirts, etc.) to scholarship.

In education, incentives have traditionally been a grade or points conducing toward a grade or credit. They may also be some other form of recognition or special privilege. Educators always need to find more potential rewards in the nonmaterial. This calls for some imagination.

Information

While a fact was originally something done (from the Latin, factum), a done deed, information was a mental construct—giving form to the mind or character. The earlier use of the word information was for facts that have been integrated into a system of thinking (now called a paradigm;

see Paradigm, Paradigm Shift). Over the course of time, our sense of the word has become more piecemeal, synonymous, according to Webster, with news, intelligence, facts, data.

The word *information* has a long-standing association with the language of officialdom ("for your information"; "this is to inform you that . . ."). Information is something one chooses to use and act upon—or not. In everyday life, FYI (for your information) is almost synonymous with NBD (no big deal).

The academic world has always been a storer and dispenser of neutral, but potentially useful data. Business needed the information explosion to persuade it that information is potentially profitable.

In electronic times, information has come to mean the transmission of signals or impulses. Like a subatomic particle, this information is vital to our universe, yet not directly perceptible or intelligible to human beings. We are all nervously energized, in short, by minute impulses that are meaningless to the unaided human nervous system.

This is the core reality of our information age: much input concerning which we await understanding.

Information Age

The information age, the name of the human era at the turn of the twenty-first century, is roughly equated in the popular imagination with learning or knowledge explosion. The assumption is that information equals learning and knowledge, and the more, the better. The more precise meaning of the term, however, has nothing to do with knowledge content, but rather, refers to the sudden wide accessibility of electronically stored and transmitted information.

The business world clearly understands this specialized, technological meaning, to which a whole set of values and issues accrue. These include the following.

SPEED. (a) Since information itself is transmitted instantaneously, the value of instant gratification, advocated in other aspects of our culture, is reinforced by our technological reality. (b) Organizational survival depends on speed of delivery, going from concept to loading dock faster than the competition. Fastest is best.

EGALITARIANISM, EMPOWERMENT, PARTICIPATION. All of these values extend from the universal accessibility of electronic information. It can't be monopolized by the power elite. The business gesture of pushing decision making down in the organization may, in some cases, be making a virtue of necessity, the best of a bad deal.

KNOWLEDGE WORKERS. This appears to be the other side of egalitarianism. Technological knowledge is power. Therefore, there may be developing, many argue, a two-class system consisting of highly paid knowledge workers and the drones/school dropouts who sweep up at night.

OVERLOAD; OVERCHOICE; FRAGMENTATION; STRESS. These (along with electronic surveillance and the lack of privacy) are the less-attractive aspects of the information age resulting from too much, too fast for the human nervous system or the social organization.

For the most part, the educational response to the information age, ironically, has been to de-emphasize, even discount, information, facts, and content knowledge on the grounds that these trivial details are quickly surpassed. The feeling is perhaps that no information is better than out-dated information. Educators are endeavoring to teach instead thinking skills. Whether it is possible to learn to think—in the abstract, but about nothing—is an experiment still being played out upon the minds of our children.

Initiative

For educators, initiative is a quality that resides in people. They show initiative by inventing, planning, and starting ideas and activities on their own, without direction or being told to do so.

Business uses the word in this sense, but it also calls whole organizational efforts or planned programs "initiatives." Similar to military attacks or campaigns, they are often so large and ambitious in scale they can scarcely be linked to a single individual. The word—fundamentally meaning beginning—emphasizes the importance of the preliminary splash. When an initiative fizzles out, it may be more compatible with the corporate culture to initiate something else than to try to find, salvage, and recycle the spent cartridge.

Input

Input is data or information put into a machine. In itself, it may not be meaningful or useful; meaning and use are identified somewhere else, as part of another process. Faith in ultimate applicability is remarkably widespread.

77

I

Like *feedback*, *input* is an originally mechanistic and emotionally neutral term often applied to human beings as an attempt to defuse (or make less emotionally intense) the exchange of perceptions or opinions. Input occurs prior to an action or decision and may be ignored; feedback follows an action or decision. It, too, may be ignored. Both educators and businesspeople rely on these principles.

Integrity, Academic Integrity, Integrated Curriculum, Integral

In its old-fashioned sense of moral wholeness, the word *integrity* seldom occurs in either business or education. However, our longing for the meaningful cohesiveness of parts to wholes and words to action is apparent in the many derivatives of *integrity* in both fields.

Academic integrity usually boils down to "no cheating, no plagiarism." In some schools, it also means the maintenance of academic standards. At the higher levels of academe, academic integrity in research and experimentation means preserving the purity and clarity of results, uncompromised by carelessness or special interests.

An integrated curriculum is a plan of study that attempts to bring together various disciplines through application to a broad topic or problem. The idea is to avoid fragmentation of knowledge and skills along traditional subject lines.

In business, one frequently encounters the word *integral*, especially in the phrase, "an integral part of the business." This phrase is usually designed to show that some seemingly frivolous and often people-centered activity really is conducive to profit.

As for the moral meaning of integrity, the honesty issue is more or less subsumed in business under ethics. When it comes to dealing and trading, the business world prefers a legalistic code of specific rules over the holistic approach. In like manner, schools are far more apt to adopt honor codes than to make controversial judgments about the integrity of individuals or the institution. In private and in their faculty lounges, teachers, of course, make these judgments continually, but they know better than to bruit them about.

◆ ◆ ◆

Of Parts and Holes

78

If Marshall McLuhan was correct in predicting that instantaneous, electronic communication would turn our planet into a global village, then there must be global village idiots. I believe we're making strides in both respects.

I'm very thankful not to be a politician. If politicians said too often, "I don't know yet, I have to think about it, let's wait until all the facts are in," no one would think they were competent. It was probably a lot easier to be in politics back when you had to wait for the winds to be in the right direction to get the news. You had a lot of time to think of your answer; no wonder people used to seem more articulate.

Now, of course, politicians have to respond to everything the moment it happens. Is the dictator in or is he out? Who was cheating whom? Who's the freedom fighter? (Does the freedom fighter mean the person fighting for or against freedom?) These are details they must more or less fake, but what we have lost in eloquence, we have perhaps gained in the art of temporizing. If idiots are people whose information consists in little, unconnected pieces, a lot more of us are idiotic now.

Yet there is something to be said for learning to live with partial views.

I knew someone who lived in an apartment building and was tormented day and night by the sound of a person in another apartment attempting to play the oboe. The oboist practiced long and practiced daily, but never got beyond squeaky, out-of-tune scales. My acquaintance grew enraged to the point of contemplating pounding on the offending door and "punching the guy out."

"But then," he would always go on to say, "I keep thinking, suppose it's some poor guy in a wheelchair, and playing the oboe is his only pleasure in life." So he never did anything about it. That's what happens when you consider that you don't have the whole picture: you're forced to set aside the pleasure of self-righteousness.

Then, too, parts are often more attractive than wholes, as the following may illustrate.

Some time ago, I was sitting on the third floor of a college library in a seat that overlooked a gigantic construction site, dubbed by students "the hole." As is often the case, though a wooden wall had secured the area since the initial excavation, the builders had, as a courtesy, cut a little square window in one part of the wall through which passersby could satisfy their curiosity.

It was most amusing to compare the Lilliputian size of the window with the vastness of the scene it was supposed to reveal. And it was just as amusing to see the hole's-eye view of the world.

First, a large face with dark glasses filled the space, and its matching hand clutched one corner of the window. It was the face of a plump man, and his interest was so persistent that when a girl with blonde bangs pushed into the space and he let her look, his hand remained grasping the corner. It was as though the loss of perception had only increased his tenacity.

The blonde bangs bobbed around quickly and withdrew. Immediately, the glasses poked back into the window to rejoin the hand. At length, though, the glasses reluctantly moved on, but the hand still lingered a moment, dragging along the bottom of the window until it, too, disappeared. The window became a blank sheet again.

A little later, a dark-haired head emerged. He kept a respectable, almost furtive distance, and surveyed the full angle of vision in a single, sweeping motion, as though either reluctant to spend much time there or afraid he'd be caught peeking.

I wondered how many of these spectators knew that what they were straining to see in part was visible in full from another vantage point. But perhaps, if they had had my seat, they would have likewise ignored the panorama and restricted their sight to the monitor-like square in the wall, finding a glimpse more alluring than the whole.

♦ ♦ ♦

Intelligence

Most people are confident that they can recognize intelligent or smart individuals, and more often than not, there is widespread agreement in such judgments. Beyond that, many also distinguish between being street smart and book smart. Again, most find it easy to grasp and agree on this distinction.

When it comes to the broader concept of intelligence, definitions are harder to agree on or even express. Luckily, the concept is of concern almost exclusively to educators—first, because they value the readiness or ability to learn (a classic definition of intelligence) in and of itself and hope to foster it, and second, because they are always concerned with potential as well as performance. In business, once a person is hired, the only concern, as in the world at large, is in performance. (See Aptitude [and Potential].)

The general public equates intelligence with IQ, a score on a particular type of test. Topics under debate among psychologists and educators are whether such scores adequately reflect all forms of intelligence, to what extent they really measure the ability to learn, what types of achievement they actually can predict, and how much they depend on heredity and environment. The common distrust of these tests is often expressed as, "So-and-so is smart, but doesn't test well."

One point most do agree on is that IQ tests measure the qualities and abilities our culture has historically considered important, whether all professional performance depends on them or not. And no matter how many types of intelligence experts posit, a common denominator seems to be a link between the ability to recognize relationships and patterns—that is, to process, integrate, store, and retrieve information—and the ability to learn.

Interaction (and Interface)

Interaction, of course, is a word widely used in all fields to mean the action between two or more people. Social scientists like it because it is broad and nonjudgmental. (See Nonjudgmental.) Before it gained such popularity, people used to be more specific and described what they observed by using such terms as *talking, fighting, carrying on, flirting,* and so on.

Interaction does not occur between people and machines. What goes on between them is called interface—that is, they sit impassively and stare at each other. However, machines that are programmed or designed to play more dynamic roles are called interactive. Humans, by contrast, are rarely called interactive, though they may be praised as proactive, ad-

81

monished as reactive, or admit to overreacting. Interactive humans are called responsive, which is to say, they listen.

Interdisciplinary

In academe, knowledge that is not fragmented, monopolized, or confined by specialists is called integrated or interdisciplinary. Business organizations in which knowledge and decision making flow readily from one person, department, function, or division to another are often called seamless.

Such terms imply that fragmentation is the normal starting condition; the goal is to reassemble Humpty Dumpty to the best of our ability.

Interest

At its core, this word has to do with a relationship (literally, "to be between"). Interest really isn't intrinsic to a topic itself; it's in how one perceives it. The job of the teacher is to develop the relationship between student and subject.

The business concept of interest stresses the relationship between self and purse. To have an interest in something means a stake or investment—hence, interest also usually implies self-interest, or "what's in it for me." (See What's In It for Me? [WIIFM].)

Looking Ahead

To pursue a discussion of fragmentation and integration, parts and wholes, see the questions at the end of chapter K.

I equals Integrity

J gets the Job

Jargon

Jargon is the word outsiders apply to the specialized language that has developed in a particular profession, organization, or group. Outsiders consider this language intentionally secretive, obscure, or deceptive. Inasmuch as the social sciences often focus on widely accessible human experiences, their languages are often ridiculed for making the plain difficult. Educationese, psycho-babble, business-speak, and business babble are expressions of that criticism.

The insiders who habitually use such language do not consider it jargon. For them it's a shortcut for referencing key concepts and shared experiences. Most human groups (including couples and families) quickly evolve some subspecies of language to express their unique perspective. Just as quickly, they regard it as self-evident.

Any prefabricated language that doesn't require thought soon impedes all thinking. Like stimulants and hallucinogens, then, jargon is both natural and subject to abuse.

Job

Generally, a job is considered much smaller in scale and more specific, and restricted, in responsibilities than a career. In business and schools (as well as sports, war, and politics), the word *job* is often used interchangeably with *assignment* or *task*. It is something one is given and which one completes, as in a job to do. One may look for, find, and lose a job, but one rarely chooses it. One chooses only a career.

The poor and disadvantaged get job training; the rich and middle-class get career planning.

Just-in-Time

In manufacturing, just-in-time refers to the practice of deliberately allowing supplies to run down until the exact moment they are needed. It's a way to enhance speed and flexibility, while cutting inventory carrying costs. Some quality improvement and employee involvement efforts also employ just-in-time training, which is instruction delivered at the very moment employees identify the need for it. This heightens the motivation to learn.

In the field of education, teachers disapprovingly call such practices last minute. Their job is to teach students to anticipate consequences and plan ahead.

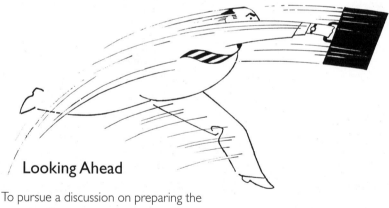

Looking Ahead

To pursue a discussion on preparing the young to live and work in society, see the questions at the end of chapter P.

K must be Knowledge

Knowledge

Knowledge implies both a profound grasp of abstract principles and an intimate command of significant detail. It does not necessarily imply an ability to act with or upon that understanding.

Educators often find it useful to distinguish among knowledge, skill, and understanding. When used as part of this triad, *knowledge* refers to the information base. *Skill* is the ability to carry out useful tasks even (and in fact, often) in the absence of any knowledge. *Understanding* is the total grasp of the subject and of its applications.

Whether the knowledge workers of the information age possess knowledge itself or merely have the skill of working with (processing) knowledge remains ambiguous in the literature of our times. (See Skills; Understanding.)

◆ ◆ ◆

Reflections on Memory and Imagination

As a human faculty, memory has suffered a great decline in prestige since the ancient Greeks considered it the mother of the Muses, or source of all artistic and intellectual inspiration. In Renaissance times, the art of memory was so highly esteemed that elaborate systems were devised for cultivating it, not only as a tool of eloquence (and thus of service to the state) but as a source of magical powers. Even now, there are large segments of our population whose early schooling included many exercises of the memory.

Yet for most of our contemporaries, such activities are dismissed as mere rote learning, the proper province of an unimaginative machine. It is not unusual for people to view a good memory as a paltry substitute for imagination. Such an opposition is peculiar, for in truth, the two faculties dwell very close together.

To be sure, there are all the things we learn by sheer willpower (like the multiplication tables) or by the jingling sounds that have a kind of magical appeal of their own ("Thirty days hath September, / April, June, and November"; "Happy, happy children we, / Now we know our **ABCs**.") But mostly what we remember lives in our minds because of sounds, pictures, and associations nourished by imagination.

Many years ago, I noticed I had a tendency to transform historical dates into specific places in my mind, often entire scenes, as in movies. (Perhaps this mental habit comes from the old "stage of history" metaphor.) Take the year 1588. Instantly, I see a parchment yellow map of Western Europe, with water painted a blue gray. The camera of my mind moves up from Spain and starts focusing on England and the English Channel, moving in closer and closer. Then, we break into action, the scene is a clamorous English town, where Queen Elizabeth appears on a fat white horse, and so on. That's all 1588 to me.

And this way of picturing and imagining information isn't just a personal idiosyncrasy of mine. A favorite Renaissance device for remembering a speech, for example, was to picture a building and to walk through it in one's mind. Every part of the structure stood for a different part of the speech.

It's no wonder the Greeks viewed memory and all the products of imagination as kinswomen. Their relationship is particularly balanced and harmonious. For while imagination, with its vivid sounds, pictures, and those associations that are the tracers in the mind's filing system, enhances memory, memory provides fuel for the imagination. People like Coleridge and Freud observed in different ways that imagination (or fancy or our dreaming faculty) relies on memory, memory freed from the limitations of time and space.

Sympathetic imagination also makes people better learners—better, that is, at understanding and remembering. "To know a thing," Thomas Carlyle observed in *(On Heroes, Hero-Worship, and the Heroic in History)*, ". . . a man must first love the thing, sympathise with it: that is, be virtuously related to it." The best learners are able to set aside their own egos, interests, assumptions, histories, and personal needs. Like lovers, they forget about themselves and open up all channels of reception. And like lovers, they are unlikely to forget anything about what so passionately holds their interest. But even learning about something we may not be interested in is possible with an act of faith (or of the imagination). "Crede ut intellegas," it was said long ago; "believe that you may understand." It's not as mindless a suggestion as we moderns might flatter ourselves into thinking.

Discussion Questions

1. What aspects of the information age have increased our desire for spiritual wholeness?
2. What aspects have intensified our need for intellectual wholeness?
3. How do business and education attempt to integrate information? What else might they do?
4. What is the difference between knowledge and information? Between knowledge and skills?
5. Where and how do judgment and wisdom fit into learning in the information age, if at all? Should they?
6. What is gained when pursuing clearly defined goals and objectives? What is lost?

For Further Consideration

1. What are the strengths and limitations of experiential learning when it comes to relating parts to wholes?
2. Ask people how they expand their knowledge and know-how as adults. What background and skills enable them to do that? What do they build on? How do they put the pieces together? How do their answers compare to what works for you?
3. The questions under Hierarchy in Education (chap. H) ask who determines what knowledge is necessary and how these decisions should be made. Where do you stand on these issues?

4. How do the questions under *"Is* versus ***Ought"*** (chap. C) and Hierarchy in Education (chap. H) reflect our desire for cultural and social wholeness?

Looking Ahead

To pursue these issues, see Reason; Skills; Thinking, Thinking Skills; Understanding. Also see "Parts and Wholes" in appendix 1.

K   K must be Knowledge

L is Love of Learning

Language

The word *language* is used far less frequently in business than in education. From the business perspective, the chief language issue is communication. (See Communication.) Considerations of language as such are often restricted to the choice of words in a contract or communiqué with legal or public relations implications.

Language in education is both a broad and important term. Broadly, it refers to comprehension of, and expression through, written and spoken words in a coherent system. In America, these skills together are often called language arts or simply English. People from other countries are often puzzled as to why Americans spend so much time studying English. Educators, meanwhile, continually devise new methods for teaching language skills and debate which ones are most effective.

The importance of language for educators lies in its correlation with thinking. Thought in the absence of language is undeniably limited. For that reason—and also because language affects one's perceptions—language plays an important part in intelligence testing. This connection, in turn, raises issues of social-cultural bias or insensitivity in the assessment and placement of students.

The topic of language in education also refers to foreign and/or second languages. Here areas of contention again center on methodology, the language that is the medium of instruction, and the importance or necessity of learning languages other than one's own.

Literal-Mindedness and the Legalistic Outlook

People who are intrigued with, and attracted to, rules tend to have mixed feelings about language. On the one hand, languages seem logical: "Change the *y* to *i* and add *es*." People who love the order of language lament the passing of sentence diagramming. On the other hand, language often flies in the face of its own rules and depends on irrational images and associations for its most telling effects. For some, it may be a vehicle for fresh discovery, but for the rule-oriented, it perversely resists uniform enforcement.

Both business and education abound in people who love and count on rules, whether to follow or manipulate them. Those who have this legalistic outlook prefer the codified dimension of language most suitable to the contract. They believe that the end of communication is best served by the narrowest and least-suggestive language possible—the letter, or literal meaning, rather than the spirit. Spirit, after all, is air, suggesting nothing but wiggle room. The poet's paradox is the lawyer's loophole, clearly something to avoid.

In reality, of course, the figures of speech inherent in language can't be avoided, so we find the next best thing among the literal-minded: a strange abundance of stilted, frozen, or dead metaphors neutralized by automatic overuse. It's become a characteristic code quite different from jargon in having little, if any, professional significance. Consider end runs, flagpoles, bottom lines, ballparks, lifestyles, shooting oneself in the foot, midcourse corrections, fast lanes, cutting edges, and so on.

This business language means nothing, and yet it means everything. It shows that the user understands the language of the power club. And in having little impact on the imagination, these flat clichés are perfectly safe as verbal gestures comparable to shaking a stick.

Leader, Leadership, Leading

People in business, education, and politics, along with our general public, share a widespread belief that our nation lacks leaders and leadership. A new idea in business is that the top people in an organization should inspire by example (i.e., lead), rather than control, direct, and command, others. Meanwhile, a leading company is one that everyone else in the field copies and follows.

Perhaps when more people regard the effort of thinking as worthwhile, we will feel less need for leaders. We don't need leadership seminars; we need to understand and reward genuine thought.

Lean and Mean

The corporate world compares getting rid of employees (downsizing, getting lean and mean) to dieting, getting into "fighting trim." It would not be obvious to most educators why *mean* is considered positive. Schools try to eliminate fighting.

The corporate mind posits a world in which the have-nots are continually plotting to assault and rob the haves. If life is a fight, meanness is an asset. According to this view, the poor have nothing to give or offer; they only conspire to take (until such time as they inherit the earth).

Humble teachers, scholars, and teachers' aides find this view at odds with their personal experience. They may also question the compatibility of the premise that people are expendable with any system of education.

Learning

The Old English verb from which we got the modern *learn* actually meant to teach.

Teaching and learning are indeed hard to separate. Teaching is impossible in the absence of learning. Incidentally, to study once meant to pursue, suggesting an effort by the student. In focusing on teaching and its techniques, we easily forget that learning still requires an expenditure of energy from the prospective learner, the paradoxical result of which is usually energizing.

Good teachers love to learn. Often, that's what brings them into teaching.

Learning Experience

In education, learning experience is a circumlocution for what used to be called more directly a lesson plan, course, field trip, exercise, unit, and so forth. Its appearance in the lexicon of the field reflects our cultural belief that nonspecific language is somehow more elegant, learned, and professional than plain, direct language.

In business, as well as among the general population, a learning experience is a challenge that turned sour. Bluntly, it's a mistake from which the speaker seeks distance.

Learning Organization

Under the influence and inspiration of MIT's Peter Senge, "learning organization" has become a widely accepted expression for the new corporate ideal (*The Fifth Discipline: The Art and Practice of the Learning Organization*). Dedicated, creative, problem-solving people will work together in the lean, efficient, flexible learning organizations of the future. Because of the reality of continual change, learning will be an ongoing process. The concept has generated great excitement.

Old names for learning organizations in our culture have been schools, academies, colleges, and universities. In today's climate, these institutions don't generate great excitement.

Learning Style

For teachers, corporate trainers, supervisors, managers, motivators of all sorts, it has been useful to discover that human beings have various preferred ways of learning—favoring different senses and/or methodologies. A path less traveled is the notion that other human beings also have different teaching and managing styles and that learning to recognize and accommodate to these variations for a common good is also useful and beneficial.

Lecture

Lecture comes from the Latin for reading and dates from the time when books were rare and a public reading to note-taking students replaced the textbook.

The current low estimation of the lecture is manifest in many ways. Commonly, to give someone a lecture is to call him or her on the carpet, an official dressing down. In education, lecturing is widely considered an outdated style of teaching—too authoritarian and insufficiently interactive. Nevertheless, for certain types of learners, it remains a highly effective approach; it is the most efficient way to present information to large groups of people (in fact, many audio-video aids are merely lectures in other media); and in its higher forms, it sustains an important academic tradition of eloquence, even entertainment.

Lifelong Learner

Lifelong learning is gaining recognition as a necessary requirement for continuous improvement in business. Thriving organizations are envisioned as flexible learning organizations. To achieve this ideal, American business speaks of emulating the Japanese practice of hiring as workers generalists who can be continually retrained, rather than rigid specialists, who can only be laid off when their use has expired.

This development could have very encouraging implications for education if word got out that the real world actually values learning, as achievement, aptitude, and aptness. One might even hope that learning skills will be regarded as the inevitable by-product of having learned something, rather than as a new discipline in and of itself. (See Skills.)

Love

From time to time, one hears of people who love their jobs or their work, who love their classes, teachers, bosses, students, or their subject, field, business, or discipline. There are people who say they love learning, making things, helping out, causing things to happen. This is worth remembering. (See Motivation.)

Loyalty

It's easy to conjure up images of loyal customers, loyal employees, and loyal students with the mist of nostalgia in our eyes. Most see loyalty as a diminishing commodity in a lean and mean world. To feel loyalty, people need to feel valued and respected parts of a worthwhile whole. They must also have reasonable expectations that cause will have a bearing on effect and that promises will be kept. (See Social Compact.)

Social reformers proposing employee-friendly legislation often try to win over reluctant employers with tax incentives and the argument that the new regulations will create grateful, loyal workers. Bribery, to be sure, is a crude, yet sometimes effective, approximation of a win-win solution.

✦ ✦ ✦

The Love Question

Whether it's better for a prince to be loved or feared by his constituents

93

is a question Machiavelli raised a long time ago. When I once asked my high school students about the love/fear choice, applying it to the school setting, they surprised (and disappointed) me with their unanimous vote for fear as the most effective motivator. Their recommendation was particularly ironic, I should note, since this was a school that prided itself on being supportive, and teachers were appropriately intimidated from any appearance of harshness.

Theory has consistently informed me that love is better than fear, and this is what I believe. In *The Scholemaster*, for example, Roger Ascham, beloved tutor of Queen Elizabeth I, wrote that "love is fitter than fear, gentleness better than beating, to bring up a child rightly in learning." And for an example of the principle in industry, I like George Bernard Shaw's *Major Barbara*, in which a visitor, seeing the enlightened management treatment of workers in a munitions factory, has this exchange with the owner-capitalist Undershaft:

> STEPHEN. *Are you sure so much pampering is really good for the men's characters?*
> UNDERSHAFT. *Well, you see, my dear boy, when you are organizing civilization you have to make up your mind whether trouble and anxiety are good things or not. If you decide that they are, then, I take it, you simply dont [sic] organize civilization; and there you are, with trouble and anxiety enough to make us all angels!*

This is so beautifully rational, I can hardly believe it isn't true. Still, experience has been more equivocal.

I have to admit that though I believe I've always been motivated by a love of the good in my efforts, my early school years were in fact beset with a fear of the horrible consequences I imagined would attend any failure to do well. The fact that there were no consequences made the specter of them only the more dreadful.

And as both teacher and administrator, I haven't always found that when you treat people generously, they respond in kind. Sometimes they think they just succeeded in tricking you out of your supposed desire to detect and punish shortcomings. Besides, it's hard to establish the credibility of love and trust among those raised on fear and suspicion, as may appear in the following story.

Once I taught in a school in Texas that included corporal punishment among its disciplinary measures. One of my sad discoveries there was that for those brought up on it, physical intimidation may work better than repeated polite reminders. "Doug," I found myself saying to the big senior football player, "open that door again and I'll break your arm." To my amazement, he left it shut.

Among my classes was a section of sophomore English consisting entirely of boys, five of whom were tough American kids, and ten or eleven of whom were Mexicans who, save one, spoke no English. I spoke no Spanish.

My response to the situation was to start with the poetry section of the book, thinking that at least the poems didn't have a lot of words. For the Mexican kids, the poems provided lessons in vocabulary and usage. With the aid of pantomime, blackboard drawings, the creative use of Latin and French, and a Spanish-English dictionary, I could usually get the beginning bilingual student to understand, and he'd translate for the rest. Then they could start a basic written assignment. For the American kids, the poems were supposed to be expressions of thought and feeling and examples of the subtler uses of language. We'd discuss the poems, and I gave them written assignments.

The Mexicans were serious and motivated. The Americans were not; they were hard to handle. To make things worse, the Bad Leroy Brown of the school was in the class, a big, strong fat kid named Hank. Hank was a kind of counterculture hero, embodying redneck values. He was a master of colorful expressions of bigotry and violence. Kids feared and admired him. Teachers numbered his days: he was suspected of being smart, though he didn't work.

Of course, I was ill equipped to deal with Hank's class, but struggled on until a strange thing happened. I'd assigned Robert Frost's "A Tuft of Flowers." The poem is about two men who hayed the same field in shifts and never saw each other but who both decided to leave the same tuft of flowers standing because they were too pretty to cut. It expressed the common bond of humanity. For some mysterious reason, the poem really spoke to Hank. He participated vigorously in the discussion and wrote a long articulate paper on it. This was from Hank, who never wrote anything!

Not long after the Frost incident, the other American kids were being particularly obnoxious. One got out a mirror and angled it so the sun was shining in my eyes. I put on sunglasses and continued. Then somebody threw a spitball and a tussle broke out. The great Hank twisted in his too-small seat and half rose from the front. "Why don't cha'll jes' shet up and let her teach!" he said.

95

From that day, I never had any trouble with the class.

I put the question to you. What made the change: love or fear?

Looking Ahead

To pursue a discussion of motivation and learning, see the questions at the end of chapter M.

M is important:
Measure, Mission, Motive

Manage, Managing, Management

Managing and *management* usually mean running or controlling. So comforting is this concept of power, we keep extending its applications. We manage time, conflict, diversity, paradox, and waste. In schools, classroom management means getting your students to mind.

The history of the word *manage* suggests our unconscious minds have dwindling confidence in the ability of the human race actually to control anything. Consider the following gleanings from the *Oxford English Dictionary*, which informs us that *manage* comes from the Latin *manus*, for *hand*, and in English is influenced by the French *ménage*, for *housekeeping*.

1579.   *To conduct (a war, an undertaking)*

1586.   *To handle, wield (a weapon, tool, etc.)*

1594.   *To cause (persons, animals, etc.) to submit to one's control*

1609.   *To control the affairs of (a household, institution, state, etc.); to take charge of (cattle, etc.)*

1706.   *To bring over to one's wishes by artifice, flattery, etc.*

1722.   *(Often ironically) To be so unskillful or unlucky as to do something*

1899.   *(Colloquial) To contrive to get on with what is hardly adequate*

All things considered, maybe this decline is why corporate visionaries say that the management of the future will not manage, but will lead.

Market

Market is the noun for the prospective consumers (purchasers) of a product or service one intends to sell. It is a hypothetical group of people endowed with enormous power under our economic system. They choose what they want to buy, determine the value of their purchases, and vote by spending money. The science of finding out who they are and what they want is called marketing.

The concept of a market-driven economy seems so simple and to work so well in American business, it's too bad it doesn't apply better to American education. (See Free Enterprise.)

Marketing

Originally, marketing meant selling something that exists (bringing it to market). Later, it came to mean a systematic investigation of what should exist—that is to say, of what would sell, if it existed. In this sense, then, marketing or market research has become the handmaiden to decision making.

Institutions of learning that compete for students and regard them as consumer-customers also speak openly of marketing. They are still unlikely to have a marketing department as such, however. That function is generally served under such titles as Admissions, Development, and Alumni or External Affairs. Admissions here refers to selection rather than to disclosure. And as in cases of sex, romance, or courtship, affairs may also be called relations.

Master, Mastery

In business, as in general language, mastery refers to dominance. There are many terms for the concept in business—monopoly, leverage, controlling interest, and so on—but mastery is not one of them.

In education, the term *master* has a long and benign history. Teachers for centuries have been masters and mistresses. Nowadays, mastery is a specific approach to instruction in which students are not allowed to move to the next task in a learning sequence until they have demonstrated thorough competence—mastery—of the work at hand. The practice is similar to that of industries that halt production when quality standards are not being met.

Measurement

"If it cannot be measured, then it cannot be managed" and "What can't be measured, can't be fixed" are accepted dicta of business. When corporate leaders speak of measurement, they mean numbers.

Some progressive business thinking argues that if the traditionally discounted (note that telltale word!) side of business—the staff or people side, wants to gain power, it has to learn the numbers language of business. "Find ways to quantify and measure what you do" goes this line of thought; "justify your existence through numbers that impact the bottom line."

But in a time when attempts to change corporate culture are increasing, the observation that these things take time and may not yield short-term, measurable results has gained some support. Some in the business community are also acknowledging that the performance of knowledge workers, who work in nonlinear processes, is more difficult to measure.

No teacher would so much as bat an eye at the notion that there may be a considerable gap between change agent activity and measurable results or that the output of a knowledge worker is hard to plot on a graph.

Mentor (and Advisor)

Mentor is the business term for what academe calls an advisor. Both fields offer other counseling services and role models under a variety of names and forms. Mentors may simply advise or they may also function quite effectively as counselors or role models, just as school advisors sometimes do, but they don't have to. As is also the case with school advisors, sometimes their advice is acquired only with great difficulty and isn't much help. (See Role Model.)

Merit Pay

In business, it is now commonly accepted that merit pay doesn't work in motivating employees to improve their performance. The main problem is there isn't enough available money to make meaningful distinctions. When workers see how insignificant the supposed merit increase is, it perversely becomes a disincentive or dissatisfier. The other problem is that merit pay increases depend upon performance measurements no one trusts.

99

Still, despite the trend away from the concept in business, school reformers continually advocate merit pay as a great boon to education. Like school choice, it sounds irrefutably positive, perhaps conjuring up images of Boy Scout merit badges as rewards for good deeds.

Anyone who has had the misery of facing, day after day, a class that is not going well would immediately recognize the folly of the application of this industry hand-me-down to education. But for devotés of the profit motive, it may be difficult to grasp that teachers do not hold back on their ability to teach in order to get more money (a learning slowdown?) and they will not improve in pursuit of a monetary reward.

The main reason to pay teachers better is to convey greater respect for learning and the profession of education in our society. Money, like punishment, is a symbol that affirms social values. As for teaching, it's a performance art that thrives on external recognition and internal satisfaction. Performance problems are not cured by withholding a .5 percent raise. They're cured by coaching and support. Those who can't improve should leave the profession, as they would any other.

Metaphor

The predominant metaphors of education are agricultural, geographical, reproductive, sexual. One plants, propagates, fertilizes, (and cross-fertilizes) ideas. One nurtures the student. Students are shored up in a supportive environment. If they are removed from their natural place, they've been uprooted. They are mainstreamed and tended. The undesirables are weeded out. Teachers watch for growth and maturation. Every year there is a new crop of students. Bad students or classes are rotten, boring subjects are arid or dry, and some days are harrowing. Kindergarten is the children's garden. One studies in fields with stems, branches, and roots.

The metaphors of business, as many observe, are drawn from sport (ballpark, playing field, hard ball) and war (strategic, tactical, chief, executive officer, campaign, hostile takeover, blitz, nuke, big/hired/top gun, etc.). Sport itself is a kind of metaphor for war; one could even consider it a form of war with extremely tight rules. Business is somewhere in-between: rules clearly exist, but one of the objects of the business game is to work around the rules.

All of these activities are intensely adversarial (win/lose). War, like hunting, which it also resembles, has the excitement of real death. The death of sport and business is usually just symbolic (sudden death, making a killing).

Educators, especially administrators, who want to make a good impression on the public may, like politicians, employ the sport-war metaphor. That, after all, is our national image of success.

Mission

The idea of a mission appeals to the favorite self-image of business leaders as solitary hunter-warrior-knights. Originally a condensed version of the strategic plan, corporate missions now all sound pretty much the same—to be the best in quality; to be first in customer service. All businesses, in fact, do have the same mission: to make a profit. That is why it is called the for-profit sector. Mission statements thus consist of taking a means (service, quality) and treating it as an end (goal, purpose, mission). The truth is, quality and service are valued only insofar as they conduce to profit.

School missions also all sound pretty much the same: to foster citizenship, community, love of learning, values. None of these has anything to do with profit because schools are nonprofit or not for profit—that is to say, in the general mind-set, useless (unprofitable, profitless). Schools used to call their mission statements their philosophy, which, of course, implies far less expectation of action.

For models of service, business leaders should consult with teachers, ministers, social workers, and the average woman. For models of excellence, they should study scholars, artists, researchers, philosophers, and some kinds of athletes. For models of mission statements, schools should study business.

Students of mission statements might also note, incidentally, that most people are unable to recall them without recourse to a crib sheet. This is because sloganeering is not the same as reality.

Money

Whatever it is called—assets, gains, profits, capital, cash, resources, reserves, wealth—money is always good in the for-profit sector. Unless it is debt, one always speaks of money positively.

In the academic world, mention of money is often considered embarrassing or impolite. Work undertaken as a commercial or money-making venture is even spoken of with contempt.

Moral Education, Morality, Moral Reasoning

Business and education both shy away from the always controversial and sometimes indecent word *morality*. There are schools, though, that venture to teach moral reasoning, an intellectual and abstract approach to resolving hypothetical moral dilemmas. Those who want their children given moral or character education, as distinct from moral reasoning, do not find this an acceptable substitute. Often these parents advocate school choice to defray costs of religious and/or home schooling. (See Values Clarification.)

Motivation

Motivation can come from outside or inside an individual. The common experience in our most fundamental teachings is that motivation progresses from without to within. (One is praised for using the toilet and scolded for soiling one's pants. Ultimately, one feels an inner shame or guilt about a pants-related accident, whether anyone else knows about it or not.) Moral education seeks to advance the movement from external to internal motivation.

The business world, being for profit, has tended to emphasize the external motivators (love of money and recognition; fear of poverty and disgrace) and to attract those who think in terms of externals. In this regard, it appeals to the child ego state. The assumption that self-interest is life's basic motivator is rarely, if ever, questioned. The current corporate efforts to identify a mission or share the vision are, among other things, rudimentary attempts to switch to an inner motivating principle, as befits the mature and better educated.

Our profit-oriented society might not be so extravagant in its admiration for acts of generosity and heroism if its members could recognize how truly common these noble acts are, even in everyday life and humdrum employment. The reason this nobility goes so widely unnoticed is that, viewed through the spectacles of self-interest, such acts are mistaken for weakness, timidity, or folly, just what one might expect from the unemployed or ill-paid.

The thrust of education has always been to extend the individual out of his or her own self to an identification with the species or beyond. There is an ultimate contradiction in linking education to narrowly defined self-interest, even though gold stars, the ruler, and ostracism have been time-honored training tools.

✦ ✦ ✦

The Carrot and the Stick

The carrot and the stick are commonly accepted motivational tools. What is seldom considered is that "carrot and stick" is a metaphor equating human beings with horses (or less-prestigious equines).

I once saw a horse race on television in which the jockey had the embarrassing misfortune of falling off his mount just at the starting gun. I say embarrassing, but as I think about it, the accident probably had more serious professional consequences than mere embarrassment. Indeed, considering the vast fortunes involved and the interest of the betting establishment in the sport, he would have done well to escape with his livelihood, or his life.

But actually, I wasn't thinking about the jockey at the time. I was feeling embarrassed for the horse. He finished dead last.

The horse seemingly had every advantage in the world, being without the weight of the rider, but he ran a pretty sorry race. He let all the other horses push ahead and get rail positions. And he just loped along, going through the motions. Somehow, he seemed to lack commitment. To his credit, he did run and finish the race. That speaks well for his training. On the other hand, he could have just been following the crowd, wondering why all the other horses were in such a blazing hurry.

My point is that if this is the view of humanity that believers in the carrot and stick have, it's not a very flattering one.

People who believe in external rewards and punishments never understand people who believe in internal motivators, and vice versa. In fact, people in those two camps can't even communicate with each other, though they think they can and therefore become angry at the perversity or obtuseness of the other side.

Advanced management theory is more beneficent. It can speak with Olympian equanimity of the "rule of threes," as do Jay Schuster and Patricia Zingheim (*The New Pay: Linking Employee and Organizational Performance*, pp. 285-86). According to this view, one group of employees is always motivated by an inner principle and doesn't need a reward to perform well, one group won't do well no matter what, and the third group, in the middle, can be encouraged to do better through rewards. In the daily, gritty reality, though, most practitioners act and speak as if everyone were in the middle group. Whether people reared up under a carrot-and-stick approach can ever develop the working-for-love view is a question I'm not equipped, by either study or experience, to answer.

Personally, I'm glad mostly to have escaped the world of carrot and stick. Sometimes, even horses do. Consider Secretariat.

Those privileged to know him said there was something about the great horse that made him just love to race. There was nothing in it for him but the joy of running well. He never seemed to enjoy his retirement, even though, given the ancient tradition of equating sex and money, that was when he supposedly drew his reward for service. As I understand it, being a professional stud was not his true calling. It didn't really inspire him.

Thus, when people do something well for no discernible reason or reward, they are not necessarily stupid or naive. They may just be responding to a bugler not all are equipped to hear.

Questions to Reconsider

1. What linguistic evidence shows that our culture generally views life as a competitive sport or game?
2. What does this basic comparison imply about motivation? Attitudes toward others? How goals or values are established/set? Our measures of success?
3. What obstacles or limitations do schools encounter in motivating performance that business does not?
4. Consider the qualities that make a good person, a good

learner, a good worker, and a good businessperson. How are they compatible? How do they conflict?

5. What do your conclusions suggest about teaching and evaluating students?
6. What do they suggest about evaluating teachers?

Looking Back

Review Fair, Fairness; Flexibility.

Ns are for the Noncommittal

Needs Assessment

This is the process by which organizations identify the gap between the ideal and the actual: what should be as distinct from what is. As an early step in planning change, both the term and the process are widely used in business as well as education. The idea is that after the needs assessment phase, process participants agree on priorities and design action plans to correct the gaps and measure their progress in filling them.

Agreeing on needs, however, is not as easy as it sounds. This is because a need must be defined in terms of the desired end. It's a perception apparent only to those who feel needy and can say where, exactly, the shoe pinches. Needs assessment, then, is really a declaration of values, which inevitably take their color from the knowledge, experience, maturity, and prior value orientation of the individual. The argument, "We/I know better what you (or your organization) need than you do," is distasteful and unconvincing, though sometimes, perhaps, correct.

Note, too, that within this system, the ideal is conceived as a something that is missing—a lack or void. It can't be less than what one already has. The approach accords perfectly with a consumer outlook.

Need to Know

In the world of business and politics, as in our more mainstream culture, the operating assumption is that it is not necessary (or desirable) for everyone to know all things. Knowledge may be a guarded commodity, though the electronic age has made that more difficult. Luckily, sharing the vision is now considered good.

Educators generally do not view any form of knowledge as forbidden or off limits, nor do they think some lack a need to know. Their closest equivalent to "on a need-to-know" basis would be expressed in terms of confidentiality in the counseling domain and sequencing, stepping stones, or prerequisites in the academic one. Mostly, however, they would be overjoyed if everyone wanted to know.

Educators' belief that knowledge is good in and of itself often gets them into trouble with the public, much as Eve's did with God.

NIH

NIH stands for "not invented here" and refers to the resistance in the business world to incorporating ideas, no matter how successful, that originated in other organizations.

Educators don't use the term NIH, but the same concept thrives in education. Though centralized bureaucracies have forced public schools to conform to standard controls and regulations, teachers, attuned to individualizing and to classroom independence, are natural advocates of an NIH attitude.

In curricular matters, the abandonment of the traditional canon, clearly invented elsewhere, and the emphasis on contemporary, student-centered content could be considered a manifestation of the NIH attitude at the student level: "What isn't of my time and place is insignificant." Playing to this attitude, moreover, has clear pedagogical value. It's undeniably easier to hold the interest of people who are instructed to direct their gaze inward.

Nondirective

A nondirective leader knows the answers but won't tell. The thought is that people learn better by listening to themselves.

Nondirective leadership techniques, drawn from Rogerian counseling, are often used for special instructional interactions in both business and education. In the day-to-day reality, most leaders are unabashedly directive, telling others what to think and do. (See Nonjudgmental.)

Nongraded

Nongraded is an educational term for the kind of self-paced learning that used to be common in the preindustrial, one-room schools. Students are not grouped into uniform, lockstep, homogeneous grades; rather, they learn at their own pace. Proponents of nongraded schools argue that the system is beneficial to both gifted and slower learners. The chief problem in execution, as usual, is in coming up with clear curricular yardsticks and achievement measurements (see *Dictionary of Education*).

Business has not had anything analogous to this approach. It acknowledges only one pace, set by management, in pursuit of competition.

Nonjudgmental

Nonjudgmental has a favorable connotation for those who use the term. It comes from the same world of counseling and psychotherapy as the word *nondirective* and means able and willing to suspend judgment in order to listen to, and receive, what someone else is saying. Those who don't esteem these qualities do not have the word *nonjudgmental* in their vocabularies. Their view is that one either has and exercises judgment or one lacks it. To lack judgment is bad.

This polarity exists in both business and education, but the school world has had more supporters of open, receptive, nonjudgmental attitudes.

Nonstandard

In manufacturing, a nonstandard tool or instrument would be of limited use and a nonstandard product would be an irregular, at best sold at discount. Nonstandard, more often called not-to-standard, isn't good.

In education, *nonstandard*, usually applied to English, is a nonjudgmental term for "different" from mainstream or standard usage, but neither better nor worse. The term spares loss of face and provides the answer to, "But nobody says *whom.*"

Nonverbal

This is yet another term drawn from psychology and has become a standard part of communications courses for managers, supervisors, teachers, administrators, and people from any other walk of life. Just as the term nonstandard English acknowledges that people communicate effectively by using many forms of English, attention to the nonverbals (gestures, facial expressions, voice tone, body language) concedes that people communicate without language at all.

One could argue that there has been a steady decline in our culture in the belief, common among primitive peoples, that language is magical or sacred. (Cf. John 1.1, "In the beginning was the Word, and the Word was with God, and the Word was God.")

Norms

In common speech and thought, the norm is simply the middle. It's okay and what's expected.

The pursuit of the middle is key to setting standards in many techniques of test scoring. The well-known bell-shaped curve represents a "normal distribution curve," in which there is an equal number of scores above and below the middle (average, mode, and median, which in this case, are the same). Teachers who insist on grading on a curve rule out the possibility that all can achieve excellence or that all can fail to measure up. Normal distribution curves occasionally occur in nature; in the classroom, they are often fabrications to confirm our belief in winners and losers. (See Curve, normal probability, in *Dictionary of Education;* and see Intelligence in Robin Barrow and Geoffrey Milburn, *A Critical Dictionary of Educational Concepts*, 2d ed.)

Societal and behavioral norms are set to a large degree unofficially by common consensus as to what is in the middle. In that respect, they are relatively accepting, nonjudgmental, even, one might say, resigned. When a child defends forbidden behavior on the grounds that everybody else does it, the child is applying common social reasoning, however unwelcome the intelligence may be to the disapproving adult.

Advanced corporate thinkers have become quite intrigued with the nature of organizational norms. These are standards, values, patterns of behavior that have evolved and been rewarded most often in an unconscious, unpremeditated style. They are usually unofficial and unexpressed: simply what is—in the pristine absence of thought. They derive from the personality of the founder or other key individual(s) in the early days of an organization. Newcomers learn them by observation—or fail to learn them to their cost.

The many businesses attempting to undergo a cultural change often become conscious of their organizational norms. They may choose to strengthen and reinforce them or to alter them. As ever, change is extremely difficult. Support for existing norms is embedded in every aspect of an organization from figures of speech, dress conventions, and parking spaces to patterns in promotion, recognition, and pay increases.

The norm is the American ideal of the middle of the road. Normalcy is our spiritual home to which we long to return. The national pulse is generally taken in middle America, where there really is a place called Normal, Illinois. You could say that the appeal of the norm, like hiding out in a crowd, clashes with our pursuit of excellence, quality, and competitiveness. You could also say it's our national standard.

✦ ✦ ✦

Life Is an Essay Test
(An English Teacher Confesses)

Toward the end of each term, I realize I don't test enough. Of course, I have my reasons. I'd much rather have students write papers than take short-answer tests. Beside the obvious points that students need the practice writing and that an essay topic always seems to give greater scope for thinking, I justify my preference on the grounds that life is more like an essay question than a test.

In real life, no one ever tells you what will be on the test. You never really have a chance to prepare for it. At the same time, though, it's rarely a timed situation. You usually have a chance to consider what to do, to take a wide array of amorphous information, feelings, and experiences and give them some form that appears to be meaningful. In short, life is gray and vague, just like an essay question.

Clearly, however, my view is not adequate. I even think the most successful people are the very ones who do well on tests. They do have a way of figuring out what the questions will be. And they're fast to come up with answers—except, of course, when those people take my tests, which, through no deliberate intent on my part, are unfortunately unpredictable. (This, by the way, is the real reason I should test students more often: to give them a shot, in fairness, at guessing what I'm capable of doing to them.)

Besides, students never think they've learned anything unless they have a test on it. And that, in turn, is why most people don't learn anything from life.

Truth is, people need writers to tell them what it all means.

Discussion Questions

1. What is the value of nonjudgmental and nondirective attitudes in an adult psychotherapy group?
2. What is their value in a business organization that seeks to encourage worker participation, involvement, empowerment? In a culturally diverse business environment? In a high-performance organization or field of endeavor?
3. What place do nonjudgmental and nondirective attitudes have in an elementary school? In a high school? In a college? In a graduate school? In a department of research and development?
4. What is the difference between "better than all the others" and "the best possible"? Which represents the higher standard? Does competition necessarily determine what is best?
5. When is it appropriate to measure individual performance against an absolute standard or objective?
6. When is it appropriate to measure individual performance relative to the performances of other individuals in a group?

Looking Back

To reflect again on the issues of sameness, difference, and diversity, review the questions at the end of chapter G.

O is for Ownership

Obedience

Obedience is no longer in use in either business or education. In schools, obedience is called cooperation; in business, it's called playing ball or being a team player.

A disobedient student is called uncooperative, disruptive, or resistant. Business uses the military term, *insubordinate.* Interestingly, business does not praise obedient, cooperative, or teamlike behavior with the term *subordinate* (as in, "Joe is a very subordinate worker"). *Subordinate* is only a noun for people of lower rank who take orders. Now these same individuals are being told to take ownership.

Objective, Objectivity

As a modifier, *objective* refers to tangible, external reality; all independent observers would come to the same conclusions about its existence. This is the everyday, commonsense notion of truth and is the one that has triumphed in our culture.

Human fields of endeavor like business and education, which rely heavily on instinct and intuition to form judgments, often bend over backward to highlight the aspects of their decision-making processes that appear objective. In schools, tests that can be graded by a key or machine and require no judgment on the part of an educated, intelligent, perceptive evaluator, though of proven bias and ambiguity, to this day are called objective.

In business, scientific, and pseudoscientific writing, sentences that don't name the subject or doer (as in "It was decided," instead of "We decided") are considered more objective. Note, incidentally, how this so-called passive construction evades ownership.

Objectives (also Outcome-Based Education)

Goals are our highest aims and purposes; objectives are the smaller, more measurable units we can clock off to make ourselves feel better along the way.

The ideal in business is to have a clear hierarchy of goals and objectives. There is the business plan that articulates the ultimate end and generates a handful of critical success factors (or other such expressions)— those actions absolutely necessary to achieve success. Based on this information, units, departments, teams, and individuals (as part of their performance goals and objectives) identify their specific share in realizing the desired results. Many schools and educational systems also have or are striving to create an integrated view of what they are trying to accomplish and how all the individual pieces will contribute to it. Variations on this are called outcome-based education (OBE).

In education, many greeted the idea of observable, measurable, behavioral objectives—learning objectives—as a breakthrough. They provide a way to determine achievement in an absolute sense: all may successfully accomplish objectives, or none may. The artificial distribution curve or competitive measures are removed. Well-chosen learning-objective verbs can even spell out the means of evaluating the learning.

As with almost everything else in academe, all of this is subject to dispute. Those who resist formal learning objectives on principle think they trivialize education or are not equally suited to all disciplines (see Robin Barrow and Geoffrey Milburn, *A Critical Dictionary of Educational Concepts*, 2d ed.). Others simply have trouble grasping the concept; what, they ask, is so important about a verb?

O-J-T

Learning objectives can be dismissed as academic in the world of on-the-job training. In O-J-T, the objectives are always behavioral: to be able to perform, and therefore retain, one's job. The motivation for success in O-J-T tends to be high.

Oversee, Oversight

To oversee always means to supervise, no matter what the circumstances. In business, though, oversight, as in "to have oversight" also means to direct, supervise, and be responsible. In education, oversight is something one failed to remember or attend to; an oversight is something one overlooked.

Generally speaking, these differences are in character with the personality types drawn to the two professions. Businesspeople are more likely to blame or accuse others (in psychological terms, *deflect*). Educators are more likely to internalize blame and feel guilty (*introject*). Persuading teachers to take ownership is not difficult.

Ownership

In popular slang and group therapy, to own something has come to mean to acknowledge and take responsibility for something. Declaring ownership is a step toward maturity and away from childishly blaming others or passively awaiting rescue.

The association no doubt gains strength from our belief in the primacy of the pocketbook: the things we *own* must be the things we care most deeply about, in which we are most deeply invested. Ownership in this sense of responsibility has become a cardinal virtue in the newly emerging corporate value system.

When business leaders speak of ownership, they mean that they want workers to take responsibility for managing themselves, solving problems, improving goods and services, and so on. It is an interesting turn of phrase in our prevailing capitalistic environment, since in the vast majority of cases, workers receive no additional profit from taking on the burdens of ownership, and since the most fundamental decisions about their employment status still rest entirely in the hands of their superiors. The message, "Act the part of owner so you can make somebody else rich," is not an appealing one.

Besides, parents and teachers have experienced for generations the difficulties of inducing maturity by fiat: "You're almost grown-up now; you are responsible." They also often find they don't necessarily mean what they say when they command youngsters to grow up.

114

Responsibility is much more likely to be assumed than assigned. (See Accountability [and Responsibility].)

◆ ◆ ◆

High School, Workforce Preparation, and Bar Codes

One thing I learned when I moved from my home in rural and small-town Vermont to the big city of New Haven, Connecticut, is what it feels like to be an item with a bar code, being run across the scanner. I learn this every time I shop in my neighborhood's gargantuan supermarket.

Whenever I go through the checkout line, the young clerks don't look at me. They don't say hello. They don't even acknowledge my humanity. All the time that they run my purchases across the scanner, they're talking to the bag person or other checkout people about what's going on this weekend, what happened last weekend, when they're taking a break, who wants to switch workdays with whom. The scanning is automatic and in no way registers on their conscious minds.

At the end of the transaction, they don't even tell me what the total is. I'm to read it myself from the video display terminal in front of me. The machine facing the checkout lane is designed for bank or credit cards. You're supposed to type in the proper codes for automatic payment, but as a Vermonter, I stubbornly pay with cash or check. Even so, the clerks still don't look at me, say thank you, or good-bye. Sometimes, they even miss my hand with the change and receipt while they're looking at the bagger. Most customers seem resigned to the treatment. After all, it only makes sense that workers who are extensions of machines should retaliate by treating customers the same way.

Once, though, a middle-aged man kept glancing at me for sympathy, as he attempted to work his way through the system with a cart full of turkeys on sale. He had a lively, expressive face and looked as though he usually had a great sense of humor. He even managed to look marginally amused while the clerks were busy talking around and through him. Occasionally, his eyes would ask me, "Can you believe these kids?" as though he wanted to share the joke. He seemed so nice, I imagined he was buying the turkeys for some charitable event or organization.

This isn't to say he was an easy customer. For one thing, the checkout person didn't think he was allowed to buy so many turkeys and had to

115

get an okay from the manager. Then when either his bank card or the machine malfunctioned, she had to direct him to another available machine at the far end of the store.

At what the checkout person obviously regarded as the end of the transaction, the customer said quietly and calmly, almost as if to fill the void that in other times or places would have held a thank you, "You know, young lady, if I were the manager of this store, I'd fire you." He still wore a pleasant smile.

There was a silence of amazement.

"I am the *customer!*" he said with quiet intensity. "I'm a human being!"

A chill hung momentarily in the air as he wheeled off his cart of white, plastic-shrouded, frozen turkeys.

"Everybody's in such a bad mood today," the checkout girl remarked to the bag person.

The other thing I've learned from my move is that, contrary to criticism from the business community, bad high schools do a great job preparing young people for the workforce. This job *is* such schools; there really is no difference. Workers here, as there, merely show up and go through the motions. And all the time they're present, they ignore the person they're expected to satisfy, nothing they do penetrates their minds, and all their interaction is with peers about social life and getting out of work (in both senses of the expression). The work is boring, but with the characteristic resiliency of the human spirit, they ignore it.

Here, as in any school, human results require a human model.

Discussion Questions

1. How can parents develop a sense of responsibility in children? How can teachers develop it in students? How can managers and supervisors develop it in employees?
2. What factors discourage a sense of responsibility?
3. When is personal involvement in work, studies, or research good?
4. When is it a problem?
5. Should performance be evaluated solely on the basis of objective factors? Can it be?
6. Can an evaluator be objective? Should she or he be?
7. Consider Buy-in; Concern; Interest; Profit Motive. Do we really believe commitment is a matter of self-interest?

O

O is for Ownership

P means Preparation

Paradigm, Paradigm Shift

The educational use of *paradigm* for pattern or structure used to apply to declensions of nouns or conjugations of verbs. A paradigm was a model showing the correct endings to tack onto the stems or roots of the words—anything but exciting.

Since the 1962 publication of Thomas Kuhn's *The Structure of Scientific Revolutions*, it has meant the prevailing system of thought, reasoning, or methodology that in any historical period governs scientiflc research (more or less, the party line; see Robin Barrow and Geoffrey Milburn, *A Critical Dictionary of Educational Concepts*, 2d ed.). The shock for many readers was in discovering there might be more than one way to think about things, a valuable revelation to those unaccustomed to thinking about thinking (metacognition).

The notion that people may grasp a new system of thinking all at once, as a great ah-hah, paradigm shift, accounts for the aura of mysticism the word has acquired, especially in businesses seeking a fresh outlook. In academe, to say something like "Clearly, you're operating in a different paradigm" is a polite-sounding way of saying, "I think you're so stupid I don't even feel like arguing with you." Such a usage tends to defeat rational discourse.

Paradox, Managing Paradox

In educational circles, the paradox has long been a staple of the English classroom, meaning a statement expressing opposite meanings that is no less true. An appreciation of the paradox depends on an understanding that truth is complex, not a set of monolithic, either/or propositions.

The appearance of the word *paradox* in the rational world of business coincided with global and Workforce 2000 thinking and similar paradigm shifts. However, the notion that a paradox is something that merely *is* is hard for the binary mind to grasp. The expression "managing paradox" fits more into the corporate view. This suggests the imposition of a single will on multiplicity and is accordingly more palatable.

Patterns, Magic, and the Educated Guess

Human beings like patterns. I remember learning in college that in the preprint era, every time some dedicated monk copied a picture, he made it more symmetrical than his original. The point was that for a subject like botany to advance, we humans needed the technology to duplicate images exactly. The hand-drawn versions kept getting misleadingly shaped into the preferred pattern.

In addition to liking patterns, we humans also have some natural skill in detecting them. One of the more heartening observations I've read is that children, contrary to widespread belief, do not learn language simply by imitating it; they learn by formulating rules, though it's an unconscious process. If children learned by imitation, the very compelling argument runs, it would not be so common for them to say "tooths" instead of teeth or "foots" instead of feet. They make these standard mistakes not because they've heard them, but because they've formed the rudimentary hypothesis that plurals are formed by adding *s*.

Often humans discover patterns by careful observation and analysis. Often someone else clues them into the existence and nature of a pattern and then they can see manifestations of it all around them. Often people (like the "tooths"-sayers) recognize patterns unconsciously and come out with brilliant insights that seem like magic. People who recognize patterns only consciously and analytically call people who get them unconsciously illogical, intuitive, elliptical, crazy, gifted, inspired, prophetic, irrational, flaky.

One of the reasons "those who can" often *can't* teach is that they may genuinely not know how they do what they do or know what they know.

The ability to teach is itself a gift, but those who are gifted in other ways are often better coaches or critics than teachers. Knowing requires an awareness of the pattern that underlies the accidental, shifting details. This sort of knowledge often follows the act of creation or the experience of insight; it doesn't precede it. Yet conscious grasp of pattern is crucial if the knowledge is to be replicated or applied. This is also the reason institutions awarding academic credit for experience-based learning insist that the applicant be able to describe, not merely demonstrate, the learning. It's not as hair-splitting or obstructionist a process as it may seem to frustrated real-life-degree candidates.

Pattern recognition enables people to go from ignorance to knowledge by what can seem a mysterious leap. This often used to go by the words "educated guess," though it's my casual observation that the expression is less in use these days. If that's the case, I'd surmise it's because we have out-sophisticated ourselves. With all our test results and demographic data, we can successfully tailor our messages so that they never extend beyond what people already know and will therefore understand, accept, and believe. In business, communication that involves an intellectual reach is panned as poor marketing and in education, as insensitivity. I personally believe this is one of the factors that contributes to the so-called dumbing down of America. There's not even an expectation that anyone can or likes to learn by thinking and putting pieces together.

Talk about paradigms and paradigm shifts has an undercurrent of irony if not outright contradiction. The experience itself is a kind of secular epiphany that makes one's world suddenly look radically different. Like an evangelical conversion or the grasp of EST, it's the experience of getting it, that great, spontaneous "ah-hah." Then, those who don't get it (but want it) ask for the new paradigm—the manual of instruction—to follow.

Participation

Participation has long been a schoolhouse value but is new and still of marginal standing in the workplace.

Class participation, meaning controlled speech according to the rules of schoolroom etiquette, is designed to develop speaking and forensic skills, which were once the special province of leaders, in all children. The attempt to make these skills universal serves our democratic end and socializes youngsters to speak with aplomb even if they have nothing to say. The awarding of class-participation grades teaches many children that raising their hands frequently is an acceptable substitute for preparation of the assignment. At a subtler level, participation grades may also convey the message that those who do not like to assert themselves orally have nothing to contribute.

These issues also arise in the team approach in business. Real participative management is more often spoken of than practiced. It could be that business still reflects the classical stage of Western history in which the arts of speech and persuasion were required only of the ruling classes. Others must still follow classroom etiquette—namely, don't speak unless I call on you. (See Facts; Grade School, Grammar School; Prep, Private [and Independent] School; Politics.)

Pass/Fail

The pass/fail option is supposed to encourage students to experiment in studies they might otherwise avoid for fear of receiving a poor or mediocre grade. Results have been disappointing. Students seem to want gradations of feedback and evaluation.

This is hard to account for because the P/F system bears such a strong resemblance to real life, in which pass/fail goes by the name win/lose. You keep your job or you lose it. Perhaps employees would, like students, be better motivated by subtler gradations of performance appraisal made when they still have an opportunity to learn.

People

In everyday language, *people* is a general term for human beings, and that is how the word still is used in education.

In business, the word is much more specialized. One refers to "my people," meaning the employees who work for me, whom I trust, and on whom I depend. "You people" is used to address alien humanoids with whom one has nothing in common and no rapport.

Often, the business world seems to interchange the words *people* and *employees* or *workforce*. "Get your people to do something or other" means "have your employees or staff do something or other." On the other hand, when business leaders talk about educational reform, they speak of educating the workforce, as if the American people were synonymous with their employees.

120

People as an adjective, as in "people responsibilities," is a fairly recent addition to the business lexicon. It's a warm and folksy improvement over *personnel, employees,* or *human resources.*

Performance

Performance, according to Webster, means a deed or feat. In business, that's all there is: job performance and performance appraisal refer to how well one *does* one's job, and that means everything.

In schools, a performance test refers to a special (sub)type of evaluation designed for students who cannot be tested verbally—they may be too young, come from a different linguistic background, have some sort of emotional problem or physical condition limiting speaking or hearing, and so on (*Dictionary of Education*). Intelligence in the world of education is thought to include speaking, reading, writing as well as doing: verbal IQ *and* performance IQ equal total IQ.

Politics

Opinion differs about whether *politics* is a word one can use openly without shame. However one defines it, it always has to do with the allocation and reallocation of power among people. Political skills are general social skills intensified by

- *Experience within the social system*
- *The ability to use charm and/or intimidation*
- *Self-confidence*
- *Courage*
- *Intuition*
- *Willingness to ask and perform favors*
- *A gift for persuasive speaking*

Western civilization has thought these the essential skills for leaders since ancient times. This, by the way, is one reason why the study of language and rhetoric has such a strong educational history in the West.

In business, the focus shifts from productivity to politics as one rises in the organization. One moves from direct forms of making or doing things to the indirect forms—causing others to make or do them. These principles also hold for educational organizations.

Portfolio

Portfolio originally meant a case for carrying papers. Today, it most often refers to the representative works of an artist or architect or to the holdings and apparent strategy of an investor (*Webster's Ninth New Collegiate Dictionary*). Portfolios hold an array of things that can't readily be conveyed under a single number or label.

In the world of school reform, portfolios are a new device for collecting, monitoring, directing, representing, and evaluating student productions, usually in English or mathematics. They emphasize the individuality of each student and view learning as a long process. Using and evaluating them calls for more time and a higher skill level from the instructor than traditional methods. An emphasis on scores and standards is far more conducive to efficiency and uniformity.

School reformers who value real-world preparation must decide whether the world seeks sameness or difference in the next generation. Then they must prepare to pay the cost of their choice.

Prep, Private (and Independent) School

The blanket expression for prep and private schools is "independent schools." This is what these educational institutions prefer to call themselves. Historically, they have resisted proposed reforms that would subject them to national rules and restrictions. Their essence is in their separateness: independence.

The term *prep* derives from the definition of virtually all these schools as college preparatory, but it is a term rich in suggestiveness. Public schools are under fire for not preparing students for the work world that lies ahead. Teachers are faulted for knowing how to prepare students for college, but not for life. Prep schools make overt claims to college preparation in their very titles, and their official philosophies usually make additional claims about preparing their graduates to serve the larger needs of society and their station beyond.

As socializing institutions, prep schools develop in their students

- *Ability to recognize, fit into, and work around a system*
- *Smoothness or readiness to get by with style*
- *Self-confidence*
- *Insensitivity to pain*
- *Facility in grasping patterns*

- *A strong base of social connections and the tools for*
  building them
- *Verbal ease*

Prep schools do prepare students for real life but not for a workstation. (Cf. Politics.)

Problem Solving

Problem solving is a specific mental task that seems to be replacing the general term *thinking* in both business and education. In each world, the term means the same things: a step-by-step, linear process for overcoming a perceived obstruction to progress. It's a recipe for thinking that is more likely to yield the type of creativity that works within and around a system than the type that makes or perceives new systems. People who like games and rules like problem solving. (See Thinking, Thinking Skills.)

Process

As part of their common receptivity to social science influences, both business and education have become increasingly interested in process, a focus on *how* things are done and the impact of that on *what* is done. While the processing of things (e.g., mass production) has been a major aspect of manufacturing from the beginning of the industrial era, widespread awareness of social processes has come more slowly in business than in education, where lovers of psychological theory are disproportionately represented.

For those interested in human behavior, process can become more fascinating in and of itself than the mere outcome or end. This tendency gives *process* a bad name among those who are impatient and results-oriented.

Processor

Cooking, writing, and learning are admired human arts. Processors are high-speed tools for cutting and blending food, words, and facts. They are enormous aids to those who know how to cook, to write, or to learn. To those who don't, they are major producers of waste, clutter, and confusion.

The conversion of *process* into a verb for think, analyze, sort, synthesize (e.g., "I need to process that information") is yet another indication of our cultural tendency to regard human activities mechanistically. *Processor* is also hard to pronounce.

Productivity

Among educators, as among the general public, a product is something made; and being productive is being useful. Productivity is the overall condition of usefulness, which is strongly associated with the generation of useful things. It is incompatible with waste and has strong appeal to our national Protestant heritage. In industry, the productivity of a plant is its output (minus the input) of usable goods.

Once we stop thinking about goods and products, productivity is harder to discuss. How do you measure the productivity of people who generate ideas or of people who merely work with other people? How do you form Protestant judgments about their relative usefulness? Besides, our talk and mental habits value "thing" productivity; our compensation and status systems reward people productivity (i.e., political skills). Often, only luck appears to reward idea productivity. Where does education fit into this scheme of things?

We measure our national productivity in terms of things produced to meet our needs and the wealth that industry generates. Wealth, in turn, creates a demand (quickly perceived as a need) for still more goods. This is called raising the standard of living.

Lifelong learning is the educational equivalent of wealth. Lifelong learners will always feel a need to learn more, whether or not it is immediately perceived as useful. This is called raising the quality of life. The question remains, is such an outcome productive? (See Value-Added.)

Profit

The profit is a tangible way of measuring past performance when it's too late to change what happened during the period under review. It's the primary point of interest in business.

Profit Motive

The profit motive attributes behavior and choices to the desire for material gain. Many people consider it the strongest motivator, intrinsically virtuous, effective, intelligent, and sincere. Others believe in a variety of equally effective motivators and see no reason why one type should necessarily yield greater intelligence or dedication than another. Some few see the profit motive as inherently debased compared to what they view as purer motives.

All of these beliefs tend to be taken for granted in arguments and never raised as a point of discussion. For example, people who state that education will improve when it is governed by the profit motive don't understand why they can't simply rest their case with such an assertion.

Prophet

A prophet is a person who recognizes new paradigms before anybody else and thus foresees the future. In the face of hostile incredulity, a prophet usually seeks refuge in the wilderness—or academe.

Discussion Questions

1. Business says it wants leaders. What suggests it really wants followers? How is our educational system geared to produce leaders? How is it geared to produce followers?
2. What do educators do besides prepare the future workforce in public schools? In private schools?
3. Do we want members of the next generation to be like each other or unlike each other?
4. Do you think there is enough coaching and feedback in business? In education? What prevents them? How do coaching and feedback differ from performance appraisal or evaluation?
5. What is involved in the ability to create patterns or systems? Recognize them? Work within them? Work around them?
6. Which abilities are in greatest demand? Which ones does our society reward most?
7. What are political skills, how can they be acquired, and how are they used?

Looking Ahead

To pursue a discussion on preparing the young to live and work in society, see the questions at the end of chapters R and S.

Q is Quality

Quality

Quality has gone by many names—excellence, zero defects, high performance, competitiveness, in business; excellence, scholarship, high standards, competitiveness, in education. The word *quality* as incantation is
associated with quality movement pioneer W. Edwards Deming, who
ultimately abandoned all use of a word he saw as debased.

Quality will be succeeded by other words because we humans tend to
confuse naming with doing. When one reasonable effort fails to meet
success, we give it a new name and try again.

Quota

A quota is a minimal quantitative target or goal set by higher authorities.
Satisfaction of quotas is often grudging. While in the realm of productivity, meeting quotas can be a source of pride, in social reform, quotas
usually imply a legislative mandate that is repressive to free enterprise.

Though there is no logical reason for the association, common usage
assumes that a self-defined quota is impossible, a contradiction in terms.
A fast way to make any quantifiable ideal unwelcome is to suggest it is a
quota.

Discussion Questions

1. When does quality represent a minimum standard? When does it represent a high standard?
2. In what situations can quality be predetermined and measured? In which ones can it come in unexpected forms?
3. Does/should education have any place for variety and the unexpected when encouraging and measuring quality? How about business?

R means Roles and Rules

Real World

The real world is everything *other* than the school world. Many structures and names exist for creating links between these imagined worlds: apprenticeships, internships, case methods and studies, practicums, role plays, simulations, co-ops, and so on. (See Co-ops).

Whenever formal education of the young diverges too radically from the everyday experience of adult society, cries go out for reform. Our unfortunate habit of accepting the distinction between the real world and the school world, however, implies one doesn't begin to live until one leaves school and that learning itself is less than real. Such sentiments are not only untrue, they devalue learning and teach the young to hold it in contempt.

Reason

To reason means to choose, sequence, distinguish big from little, analyze, synthesize, draw inferences or conclusions, use logic, and so forth. As a noun, it is an (imagined) internal property or faculty of the mind and refers to the highest cognitive power—as in, "Man's reason raises him above the animals and places him slightly below the angels."

Both business and education are more likely to use the noun *reason* to mean an explanation or excuse. It answers the question "Why?" and its effectiveness is measured less by its conformity to some standard of truth or internal logic than by its ability to satisfy the desire for an answer.

Reason also means "my way"—as in, "I think I can get him to listen to reason."

Reasonable, Reasonable Accommodation

Reasonable means conforming to reason, consistent with a larger rational whole. Webster glosses it as moderate or fair.

Employers have voiced skepticism that human beings can possibly agree on, let alone legislate and enforce, what is reasonable. According to the Americans with Disabilities Act, employers may not discriminate against hiring any disabled person if, with reasonable accommodation, the person can perform the essential functions of job. The phrase causes concern.

Educators, by contrast, have been accommodating for (and to) disabilities for a long time. In fact, disability in some form has always been their raw material. Teachers may also be more practiced in reaching consensus as to what is reasonable. It's a necessary survival skill to avoid classroom mutinies.

Recommendation

The recommendation is in the academic world what the reference is in business. The fact that candidates for positions choose those who will assess their past performances would seem to slant the review in the candidates' favor.

Whether writing or speaking, the people put in this situation can be sued for saying both too much and too little. It's become increasingly difficult for anyone to share an honest evaluation of someone with any other human being.

References

In business, references are people willing to talk about a job candidate, presumably to back up the candidate's application. The references may or may not know the candidate well.

In academe, references are printed materials, usually to back up the opinions or information provided by an author. The author may or may not know the references well.

Restructuring (and Re-engineering)

Restructuring means both more and less than it suggests. At root, it simply means creating a new structure, reorganizing. But inasmuch as the very identity of a business comes from its organization (organization, after all, is one of the generic names for a company, firm, business, or corporation), reorganization can be extremely traumatic. Also, it seems the new structure always calls for fewer employees. Thus, *restructuring* is often a business alternative for *downsizing* and its euphemisms. Sometimes that's all people mean by the word.

Because *restructuring* is an important word in business, it has also become important in America, a pompous word for change or reform. When educators write and speak of restructuring the schools, they can mean a variety of innovations, some of which may actually have to do with structure.

Re-engineering is a newer business term for restructuring. It's a this-time-we-really-mean-it term for those who didn't get it the last few times around or who are more comfortable with mechanistic models for change. If it plays well, it will probably be applied to schools.

Résumé

For most of the English-speaking world, the résumé is a summary of one's work history, experiences, education, and qualifications produced as part of a job application. Only in the higher reaches of academe is such a document called a curriculum vitae, which is Latin for "course of life." (For the significance of the metaphor, see Career; Curriculum, Curriculum Vitae.)

A well-constructed résumé lends a coherence and linearity to one's history worth almost any price. It makes one's life seem planned. No wonder companies that have just gone through a restructuring often hire "outsourcing" firms to help displaced workers with their résumés.

Some business leaders have suggested that the record of high school graduates be cast in the form of a student-generated résumé instead of the old transcript of fragmented courses, grades, and scores.

Arguments in favor of this practice are that it would force students to define a goal and integrate their experiences with that goal in mind, and it would be shorter and easier for a prospective employer to read and understand than a transcript or portfolio.

Arguments against it are these: it's not reasonable to expect a seventeen- or eighteen-year-old to identify a single purpose toward which his or her whole education was heading; to do so tends to undermine the goal of education, which is to expand possibilities, not restrict them; and perhaps, resulting résumés would have about the same degree of authenticity as present-day adult ones.

✦ ✦ ✦

Just Lucky

There's no question that it's most socially beneficial to concentrate on hard work, perseverance, and even social skills, as components of success. Everybody also believes in talent, though it's less polite to talk about something that seems innate. Hardly anyone pays attention to the phenomenon of good luck, which our culture forbids us to acknowledge. Still, it's worth some thought, at least on the sly.

Taking a stab at something that's long interested me, I'd say lucky people are people who don't worry. One possible explanation is that people who don't worry are freer to notice things that come up spontaneously around them. Worriers are too busy concentrating on "the plan" to see opportunity. Further, having bad luck reinforces the tendency to worry, while having things go well reduces it. This is why luck, good or bad, tends to run in cycles. Whole families may have good or bad luck, but the same families often have lucky members and unlucky ones, with everyone knowing which is which.

People who want to do well and who don't see an obvious link between their own efforts and the results often believe in—and even have— luck. Entrepreneurs tend to be lucky, at least at first. Hyperactive children and people with learning disabilities are also often lucky (if they aren't accident-prone). Sometimes what they consider luck is really a talent they have but aren't aware of.

Generally speaking, rich people have good luck and poor people have bad luck. Whenever I've ridden in someone's luxury automobile, I've known I couldn't possibly be in an accident, no matter how bad the weather. If you're ever at sea and the ship is in trouble, my advice is to look for somebody rich to stand next to.

It's important, though, to keep clear about the sequence of these things. Luck often helps people to become rich or successful, but luck is not by any means a precondition for success, nor does it necessarily lead to success. In fact, a lot of people who are most self-consciously lucky are also society's losers. Think about the expressions "the luck of fools" or "happy-go-lucky." Society has always envied and at times resented such people but never particularly wished to emulate them. Worrying and planning make for solid citizens, just not lucky ones.

The trick about luck is that it isn't willed. Worriers, who have bad luck, imagine they can control things if they take the right precautions. They try to look at everything, much of which includes what has gone awry. The conviction that they can control things also leads to a lot of frustration, and that, in turn, is another big source of bad luck. This is because frustration and anger make people rigid.

Lucky people are fatalistic. They don't think they can control anything. They wait for something to happen, and they don't worry about it if it doesn't. This gives them a greater capacity for enjoying life's small pleasures that many mistake for good fortune.

Of course, it's often argued that we make our own luck, especially by psychologists, authors of self-improvement books, and facilitators at human-potential-type retreats. I see their point but remain skeptical. There's something contradictory about *trying* to be lucky.

On the other hand, there's no denying bad luck can be willed. In fact, the thing you most worry about tends to happen, often with a vengeance. Maybe worriers unconsciously want to confront what they most fear as a relief from worry. Maybe they unconsciously know they give off some emanation to which even inanimate objects and the animal kingdom respond; in other words, they have reason to worry. Who knows?

We're brought up on the tortoise and the hare, the grasshopper and the ant, but real life is much richer in possibilities than the nursery. We pay our most consistent lip service to the hard-working ant and the persevering tortoise because we know we can count on them, even though they aren't very appealing as personality types. We want our schools, once again, to produce more of them. Yet we heap our most lavish societal rewards on the talented hare and the charming grasshopper, for we can't help admiring their joy in life. Of course, whether or not they hold on to those big rewards should stem, as the fables teach us, from principles of character. Sometimes, though, it might just be a matter of luck.

✦ ✦ ✦

Rightsizing

Rightsizing is the optimistic term for reducing the workforce, getting lean and mean. The word implies there is a kind of Platonic ideal size for each business and the task of management is to find and hold it.

Most educators feel they know what the right size is, but few schools can afford to rightsize. Therefore, they have no use for the word. In fact, if the student is the customer, schools are sometimes in the strange position of having too much business. Then it's not called success, though, but overcrowding.

Risk

Risk is possible danger that is recognized in advance, calculated, and consciously chosen or avoided. In business, where the highest potential returns usually entail the greatest risks, risk taking is a form of gambling, presumably based on a combination of information, rational principles, and instinct.

Given our national preference for remembering only success and our impatience with rational processes, risk taking has become a sort of cultural value in and of itself. Commencement speakers frequently advise graduates to take risks without any accompanying commentary on first evaluating them. Adolescents seldom need this advice.

In the everyday world of schools, at-risk students are those in danger of academic failure or other social aberrations. Educators don't embrace risk; they worry about it.

Role

Business has been intrigued with the concept of organizational roles as something distinct from job, department, or assignment for some time. This role may emanate from the individual's actual personality, identity, or style. Or, as is implied by the acting metaphor, it may be something played by a team member carrying out an assignment. Management workshops, seminars, and professional development books that enable people to identify their own and others' organizational roles and styles have the curious effect of making everyone feel affirmed, no matter what the finding. It is always comforting to have a label to go by and to belong to a recognizable group.

Though teachers often focus on individual, even idiosyncratic, differences among students, the social mission of education is to prepare the young to assume a sanctioned role in society. The nature of that role is too often unexamined. The tendency to take it for granted, in fact, accounts for much of the passionate anger in education debates.

133

Role Model

Both the words *role* and *model* refer to a manifest pattern. Role model is a model of a pattern. It really doesn't make much sense when you stop to consider it, but we seem stuck with it.

Like athletes and ministers, educators have been decreed role models, apparently by public acclamation. This means they don't just do a job, they assume an identity which they are expected to maintain at all times. Few other professions make this same demand. Teachers, athletes, and ministers are supposed to demonstrate through every word and action how human beings ought to behave. Their nature, like Shakespeare's in Sonnet 111, is "subdu'd / To what it works in, like the dyer's hand." (See Identity.)

The closest equivalent in business to the role model goes by the name of mentor. Many people want to have mentors; few want to be them. The reasons for this inconvenient asymmetry aren't hard to find. Ask a teacher. (See Mentor [and Advisor].)

Rules

The difference between people who follow rules and people who break them is not as great as the difference between those who use rules as a way of thinking and those who don't.

Studies of children at play analyzed by psychologist Carol Gilligan (*In a Different Voice: Psychological Theory and Women's Development*, pp. 9–11) noted that boys tend to favor games with detailed and complicated rules. When an argument breaks out, the boys engage in elaborate disputes and negotiations over the rules, but the game continues. Girls favor simple, turn-taking games with few rules (like jump rope and hopscotch). When an argument breaks out, the girls quit the game and do something else. Continuing the relationship is more important to them than finishing the game or determining winners and losers.

Business is habitually compared to a sport because it is a "boy" game. (See Metaphor; Athlete.) Rules are critical to the thought process. One uses them in part to anticipate moves of competitors and design counterstrategies. They provide the bounds that give meaning to the game. Even success in bending, breaking, or sidestepping a rule would suddenly lose all impact if the rule itself were voided. As in asymmetrics, rules provide the resistance and necessary tension that build mental strength.

Business leaders complain about excessive rules, especially government regulations. But this constant protest shouldn't be mistaken for antipathy to rules. Rules set certain people up to be losers, without whom there could be no winners. Even war itself has clear conventions and codes, and the opposing forces, their thick volumes of regulations.

Parents should note that the more competitive the school, the more rules it usually has. People with internal motivation—and true learning organizations—thrive best with few.

✦ ✦ ✦

Uniform Lessons for Life

Private schools have led the way in using uniforms and dress codes to prepare the young for real-world success. Everyone could benefit from studying the lessons of these codes.

Now admittedly, many of the advantages of uniforms and dress codes are unique to private schools. For example, a uniform provides an outward sign that the children belong to a specific, recognizable community, inclusive in and of itself, yet exclusive of others. It's chastening, as befits the artificial world of privation that is the private school experience, and suggests Christian humility and egalitarianism. In its slightly Spartan quality, too, it emphasizes that private school is where one's children are sent for discipline, just as obedience schools are for one's dogs and special trainers for one's horses. Dress codes can keep daughters looking young and sexless. They can steel sons for a life in collar and tie, the very yoke and harness of civilization. Some even assert that it lessens the competition for clothes.

Of broader applicability, though, is the capacity of the code to teach that most essential skill of functioning within and around a system. This it does with ingenious variety.

How does a mere dress code accomplish this? Consider the following:

First, the code requires a mastery of a complex set of rules.

Second, it sharpens the legalistic faculties—that is, the code may neglect to say both socks must be the *same* solid color; it doesn't specify width or angle of collar or lines or depth of neckline; it may leave countless ambiguities regarding the interpretations of shades; it leaves to subjective interpretation the point at which a turtleneck shrinks to a crew neck or expands to a cowl neck, and so on. Every year, in fact, the dress-code section of school handbooks tends to grow longer, with more and more things allowed, and more and more specific items prohibited. And

135

every year, the current handbook addresses the previous year's aberrations, out of fashion by the time the new book goes to press. Last year's combat boots are this year's baseball caps, so to speak. (Or is it the other way around?)

Third, it directs attention to appearance and gives appearance great symbolic value. This is key to the politics of success. Also it develops both the lexicon of appearance and the skill to judge others at a glance.

Fourth (and contrary to official rationalizations), it stimulates competition. The principle of being best at fitting in is here translated into looking either best or most outrageous without getting punished.

Fifth, it provokes conflict, which is widely perceived to heighten intelligence.

Sixth, distinctions are so arbitrary that all thought of the purpose behind the code is forgotten: this is good training for an unquestioning acceptance of traditional values and common practice.

Seventh, and for the same reason, it dissociates the concept of law from the concept of social principles or responsibilities.

Eighth, and by extension, it teaches students that the only reason to follow a rule is to avoid punishment and, conversely, that if the odds of getting caught are poor, there is no reason to follow a rule. This is helpful in forming attitudes about business and taxes.

Ninth, it gives students, parents, alumni, and faculty something to criticize. Most forms of negative criticism imply superior intelligence, while any positive proposal runs the risk of being criticized in turn.

Tenth, it serves as a barrier that diverts attention from such awkward, unpleasant, and controversial problems as self-doubt, loneliness, learning difficulties, too fast a social scene, health problems, eating disorders, death of loved ones, separation from family members, and parental abuse, alcoholism, divorce, neglect, or unrealistic ambition projected onto the child.

Some say a dress code also provides adolescents with a safe form of rebellion. There may be some students, the argument goes, whose potential susceptibility to pot may be satisfied instead with an unauthorized sock. I personally have no proof that the behavioral steam engine functions this precisely.

One thing I can say for sure is that the students' wild experimentation in mess and disorder generally ends with graduation; it seems they only feign slovenliness while at school. At graduation, the seniors each year shake off their beggarly disguises and step forth to embrace the values and roles they never, in their hearts, forsook. Whether people focus on being for or against rules is a trivial distinction as long as all focus on the same, received code.

Discussion Questions

1. Should education prepare people for the world as it is now? How good are we at predicting roles that individuals will play? How good are we at assessing their talents? How good are we at predicting the needs and dynamics of the future?
2. Review Accountability (and Responsibility). What influences our behavior besides rules and laws?

S is for Success

SAT

The SAT is an important test, though of what is somewhat ambiguous. During most of its existence, SAT has stood for Scholastic Aptitude Test. It remains the basic entrance examination for applicants to American higher education. However, its creator, the College Board, never intended it as the sole indicator of success in college, and many colleges have stopped using it. The College Board also never intended the SAT to measure the success of schools or teachers, although the public and its spokespersons are in the habit of doing so. The test has been revised and renamed the Scholastic Appraisal Test.

Critics have long said this multiple-choice, timed examination does not test critical thinking, creativity, or writing ability. They've said the content and references of the test questions give the edge of familiarity to affluent white males, the format favors personalities at ease with the gamesmanship of guessing, and much of the examination reflects home environment. Revision hasn't put these charges completely to rest.

To the extent that the test still measures self-confidence and familiarity with the cultural status quo, it might be a good indicator of real-world potential for managers of old-style organizations.

SAT Words (and Math)

"SAT words" is the name high school students, and a surprising number of high school teachers, give to English words considered too big, hard, or pompous for everyday speech. Seniors who have taken the test for the last time wonder why teachers still think it necessary to expand their vocabulary. The idea that language is a crucial instrument of thought, especially abstract reasoning, seems to be fading away in our transition into an oral, postliterate culture. In like manner, "SAT Math" refers to the level of mathematics whose only use appears to be an admissions hurdle.

Together, these two expressions bear eloquent testimony to the perceived separation of education and the real world.

Security

The meanings of *security* common to business and education concern the establishment and maintenance of physical safety for property and personnel. Business and the military also think it important to secure information, which in academe isn't considered worth stealing (unless it's going to appear on a competitive test).

The next most common use of *security* in business appears in the expression "job security," meaning a guarantee of continued employment perceived at least by the employee. (See Social Compact.) In academe, this is called tenure. (See Tenure.)

Educators reserve all other applications of the word *security* to children, who are thought to be more productive when operating with a reasonable assumption of safety rather than in an ongoing condition of fear. Periodically, this belief is also applied to business as well.

Self-Paced

Self-paced learning is useful in both business and education. Such aids as computerized instruction, audio-video tapes, even the old-fashioned workbook are obviously convenient training tools for adults who are learning while meeting other commitments. The goal is to reach a certain end result; how long it takes is irrelevant.

The same sorts of tools also appear regularly in the classroom, but the issues are more complex. Is time of the essence, or is it irrelevant? Who learns better through competition, fear, and pressure to finish by a deadline? Who is well enough motivated for more self-direction? How do you know when goals are met, or when the race is done? Is it a race at all? Which environment most resembles the expectations and needs of society: the race to finish or the quest for good ends?

While one vision of our future society has people at all ages flowing in and out of learning institutions when and as needed, permission to take an untimed SAT goes only to candidates with a documented learning disability. Clearly, our current system considers self-pacing a program for the handicapped.

Service

For many of the middle decades of this century, the once-common business reference to service all but disappeared in the United States. The faintly old-fashioned word seemed better suited to bourgeois shopkeepers and waiters (along with ministers and teachers) than to corporate conquistadors.

Then along came global competition, and prospective purchasers, with their new magnitude and potential wealth, became truly worthy of service. The very concept of a service industry was aggrandized beyond such humble functions as car repair, hamburger cooking, housecleaning, typing, and filing to include banking, insurance, financial, and communications services. "We're here to serve our customers" can be proudly voiced. It's not necessary to add, "and our turn . . . and ourselves."

Meanwhile, educators continue to serve, in their humble fashion, students, parents, communities, and society. But they've done it so long, they forget to talk about it. That enables critics to say with all the zeal of the recently converted, "The trouble with schools is they've forgotten to serve their customers."

Skills

Of the basic learning triad—knowledge, skills, and understanding—skills, the how-to component, is the most prevalent term. One doesn't read, think, or listen, for example; one uses one's reading, thinking, or listening skills. The circumlocution has many advantages as a communication tool.

First, in separating the actor from the action, it enables one to couch criticism in a nonjudgmental, depersonalized, no-fault form. "You're not using your listening skills" sounds gentler than "You need to listen."

Second, all the skills compounds convert an activity one learns how to perform into an entity one acquires like a consumer product. It seems a lot simpler, for example, to "use one's study skills" than "to study."

Third, as many trainers, educators, and supervisors have pointed out, skills are more readily presented as transferable than either knowledge or understanding, which seem bound to a particular time, place, job, or discipline.

A possibly unfortunate side effect of this last advantage is that what can be transferred from one situation to another is in reality often set aside and forgotten—in effect, lost en route. That's because it is not integrated into anything the would-be learner really values. Somewhere along the line, people must develop what one might call connecting or caring skills.

Social Compact

Social compact is the name given for the long-standing common understanding between employers and employees that as long as workers performed their jobs satisfactorily, they could reasonably expect continued employment and the fulfillment of promises of pension and other benefits. Since the recession(s) and downsizings of the 1980s and 1990s, however, there is widespread feeling that the social compact is off. Under business necessity (see Bottom Line), employers do not feel obliged to fulfill promises, a development that has encouraged a corresponding reduction in company loyalty on the part of employees.

The so-called breaking of the social compact sounds a rather dissonant note in the era embracing quality, employee empowerment and ownership, and team building. It also causes some consternation in institutions charged with socializing the young in such virtues as honesty, commitment, and effort.

Socialization

Socialization is the process in which an individual learns and takes on the norms and values of the prevailing culture of which he or she is a part. Employees must be socialized to their workplaces; new citizens to their adopted lands; children to adult society.

Whenever there is division in a culture or community about its values, there is bound to be widespread disapproval of the educational system. And to the extent that most human organizations have some gap between their overt and covert values, a socializing institution like a school will tend to raise tension. Schools reflect and heighten these conflicts; they do not, themselves, cause them.

Speed

Speed can mean velocity, how fast, in a neutral sense—as in rate of speed, but more commonly it means very fast and is an absolute good. (See Faster.) This accords with the original but archaic meaning of the word as "prosperity" or "success;" to speed was to thrive.

The ideal of an ultimate balance of speed, quality, and cost still tantalizes and eludes top business management. It also eludes educators.

Standard

In industry, there is no significant difference between the words *standard* and *standards*. What is standard—product, person, performance, procedure, plant—meets all individual standards. To become a standard of the industry is something to be proud of.

Unless they live in very poor, disadvantaged school districts, most parents would probably not say they want their children and schools to be standard. Generally, the word implies dull, mediocre, and the same as everybody else.

The socializing goal of schools is to make our citizens standard.

Standardized Tests

While the national standards issue awaits resolution, many schools across the land continue in their routine administration of common tests. These are not called standards tests, but rather, standardized tests. That means

that uniformity in the processes of administering the tests and interpreting the results (setting the standards, so to speak, after the fact, based on how everybody did) is at least as important as uniformity in the knowledge, skills, and understanding being tested.

Standards, Standard-Bearer Schools

Academic standards are something other than standard; they are higher and more varied. Most people expect educational institutions to set standards, perhaps even high standards, and minimally to meet standards. The expression

142

"national standards" in educational reform usually implies higher performance expectations, along with measurement tools, for students, teachers, and sometimes administrators and schools across the country. Community standards may suggest a supplement—or alternative—to national standards. Because of court decisions in such matters as censorship, obscenity, and pornography, "community standards" also has a connotation of local morals, values, or mores. These factors, along with antifederalist feelings, in reality often underlie objections to a national approach to school reform.

Advocates of standard-bearer schools point out that new uniform standards for students and teachers will not fulfill their apparent promise in the absence of standards for the schools or communities that should support them. (See System, Systems Thinking.)

Strategic

The word *strategic* is a repository of everything business regards most highly. It means crucial, critical, most essential to the whole. It refers to shrewd and prudent forethought on a massive scale and to bold initiatives. Its origins are in the tradition of the most intelligent, long-range, and aggressive military planning. It implies singleness of purpose—never veering off target or wavering from ultimate ends.

All organizations, even educational ones, now design strategic plans. To be taken seriously at all, one must assume this grandiose posture of world conquest.

Structure

Both business and education use the word *structure* as a synonym for *organization, system,* and so forth. (See System, Systems Thinking.) Educators also often use the word *structure* as a euphemism for discipline or externally imposed control.

Structure in a learning environment usually means close supervision and carefully spelled out, step-by-step procedures for students to follow. Students who have been neglected or advised prematurely to "do their own thing" usually benefit from a structured approach. Students who are both gifted and motivated may very well chafe at, and rebel against, this same approach; but plied with intelligence, it can salvage those who are gifted and *un*motivated. When parents say, "My child needs structure," they can mean anything from hand-holding to punishment.

143

Student Body

Schools call students in the aggregate the student body. Business calls workers in the aggregate the workforce. This illustrates the preference in education for biological metaphors and in business for military metaphors. (See Metaphor; Workforce.)

Businesspeople speaking of school reform also call students the workforce. (See People.)

Style

Style was around years before *diversity* was even recognized and named, let alone managed or valued. We have learning styles, teaching styles, managing styles, personality styles, lifestyles. Even companies and other organizations have styles. It's a breezy, easy word. We grow up hearing Casey confidently explain, "That ain't my style" while about to strike out, and we complain about systems that cramp our style, even though that appears to be the primary mission of all social organizations.

Americans grow up just assuming they have a right to some peculiarities of personal style. The one itsy, bitsy thing that can still use some improvement is learning to work with, and for, those of disparate style, whether in the classroom, the home, or the workplace.

Subjective

Since confidence in an externally observable, measurable, manageable reality is a fundamental characteristic of the business world, it has little need for the word *subjective.* The word is commonly taken to mean biased and untrue, and is most likely applied to situations in which someone's conclusions are being challenged: "That's a very subjective judgment, Smith."

The educational world makes greater allowances for subjectivity, where it is recognized as an unavoidable component of the arts and such things as creative writing. But our cultural preference for information expressed briefly and numerically, with an apparent lack of ambiguity, is equally strong in education. Short-answer tests are called objective, though no less susceptible to arbitrary bias than subjective (i.e., long-answer or essay) tests.

To acknowledge the prevalence, even dominance, of subjectivity in daily reality is to acknowledge the importance of human differences, the need to define oneself and one's perceptions clearly, the usefulness of dialogue and flexibility, and the uncertainty of life. These are inefficient, almost subversive, assumptions to operate on, so we ignore them. We don't like it when we don't know the answer, although we almost never do. We don't even know if there is an answer—just as we don't know, come to think of it, whether we study a subject or an object.

Success

In business, success is making a profit. Money and power both result from, and contribute to, further success. A successful person is one who has experienced past success and is therefore likely to continue in that mode. A successful action is one that resulted directly or indirectly in success (increased money and power) for a person or persons.

For the sake of variety, business speakers and writers often use the adjective *effective* as an equivalent to *successful*. The words are not true synonyms, however. *Effective* means what works and is likely to produce desired results. When businesspeople consider effectiveness, as distinct from success, they often get into the richer (though not necessarily more profitable) field familiar to educators. Many more values can be used to measure effectiveness than are used in measuring business success.

Public schools, colleges, and universities have tended to go with the more variable definitions of success. Should all students be socialized to accept the business definition of success as those in elitist schools are?

◆ ◆ ◆

How a Good Education Impairs Success

What is meant by preparing young people for adult life? Are they to be successful (what ambitious parents want), happy (what adolescents say they want), good people (what the moral missionaries who often end up in education want), productive citizens (what everyone ought to want)? Does the school train people to adjust to the world as it is (that is, as the world is defined by the local adults), or does it attempt to make people better (more sensitive, thoughtful, stronger, kinder) and thereby slightly improve the world?

Personally, I stumbled into an exceptionally good, though old-fashioned, liberal education. As to whether it paid off in the real world, I'd have to

145

give it mixed reviews. Here's how a good education impairs success:

1. *It teaches honesty and accuracy, which spoils a good presentation.*
2. *It stresses humility, which makes it hard to compete and sell.*
3. *It teaches one to take responsibility and not blame others; successful leaders deflect and coat themselves in teflon.*
4. *It emphasizes service, that is, a slave mentality.*
5. *It teaches one to consider all sides, including how others might be right and what can go wrong. This impairs risk taking.*
6. *It emphasizes the value of originality. This undermines marketability.*
7. *It encourages the use of imagination as a source of sensitivity to others' feelings and as a way of knowing. This impedes competitiveness and invalidates one's conclusions.*

On the plus side, one can acquire marvelously marketable skills from such an education, chief among which are the ability to listen, to remember, to distinguish big things from little things, and to sequence and integrate them.

These benefits, in my experience, have more than compensated for any lack of specific practical knowledge. One of my most memorable true-life dialogues went as follows:

STUDENT. *Dr. Kirk, are you a real doctor? I mean, if someone had a heart attack, would you know what to do?*
DR. KIRK. *I'm a doctor of philosophy. If someone had a heart attack, I could only philosophize.*

All in all, I've found that a pretty useful skill—even, I would say, satisfying.

✦ ✦ ✦

Support, Supportive

Support in the military means personnel and firepower. In business, it means people and money. In education, it means effort, encouragement, and sometimes insincerity and lying. The word *supportive*—that is, providing support—exists only in schools.

Synergy

Synergy, rather like *paradigm*, is a word that began life dully enough, simply meaning jointly working. Its first upgrade occurred when science applied it to the "correlated action of a group of bodily organs" (*Oxford English Dictionary*). Now it is a great excitement generator, expressing the idea that relationships among parts add value and energy to the whole and yield something new and different, far surpassing the sum of the parts.

The word is ideally suited for the business mindset. It sounds like *energy*, an active, can-do word if ever there was one, and it also has an aura of science. You couldn't find a more acceptable word to advocate something like magic in the hard-driving, realistic world of recovering literalists. Educators following the power-language model of business draw fresh inspiration from the word as well.

Synthesis, Synthesize

Synthesis and *synthesize* are so prevalent in educational thinking and have been for so long that the words seem dry as dust, even though they refer to the functions that characterize the human intellect at its highest level. A synthesis brings disparate elements into unity to yield a new and higher level of truth.

Up to now, it has largely gone without saying that this whole is greater than the sum of its parts or that the excitement of discovery gives off a seemingly electric charge of new energy to those who experience it. Sometimes this sensation is released as an "ah-hah!"

System, Systems Thinking

At the same time that school systems have been under attack (to the oppressed, "the System" has long been something bad), business has been considering the usefulness of systems thinking with great excitement. As change activity and our late-industrial-age hunger for wholeness grow, awareness of the interrelatedness of things spreads. The idea that organizations are systems, as complex and dynamic as living organisms, is news. Consultants tell us it isn't possible to create real change piecemeal, a little at a time, by the old scientific methods of analysis and fragmentation. It has to be done all at once, conceived as a mysterious whole.

The world will probably little note—nor even care—that teachers have always thought they were working with organisms, not mechanisms. (See Metaphor.)

Systemic versus *Systematic*

Our present-day split attitudes about systems appear in our uses of the words *systemic* and *systematic*. Both basically mean "relating to or consisting of a system." But the older word, *systematic*, has come also to mean "methodical, marked by thoroughness and regularity" and "concerned with classification" (*Webster's Ninth New Collegiate Dictionary*). In other words, it has picked up the connotations of the mechanistic, deterministic, scientific model now viewed more or less as an incorrect paradigm. *Systematic* is used for what is ossified, rote, and procedural at the cost of life. To learn about the systematic elements of an organization, ask to see the employee handbook or policy manual.

Systemic reflects the enlightened view. Anyone who wants to create real change, whether in business or in education, knows that change must be systemic to work. The connotation of this word is organic.

Discussion Questions

1. Does education prepare young people for the world as it is or as it should be?
2. Who decides that question?
3. Who decides how the world should be?
4. What is success?
5. What linguistic evidence is there of a perceived need for wholeness?
6. Review Excellence; Norms. What kind of standards do Americans seem to want?
7. Do educational institutions convey values that are not esteemed in the world of business? If so, should they continue in this practice?

T equals Togetherness

The -tainment Words

"Edu-tainment" and "info-tainment" are coinages that both business trainers and media spokespersons have claimed as theirs. The intent, of course, is to express a link between entertainment and instruction, show business, and learning.

The notion that the purpose of the arts is to delight and instruct is very old; the Roman poet Horace thought it the function of poetry. Some might say the separation of learning and pleasure is the fault of teachers who fail to capture their students' interest. Others might say that our commercial powers have indoctrinated people into overvaluing an unthinking, passive reception of pleasure at the expense of all other human activities.

It's significant that the coiners of these hybrids equate the root *-tainment* with the one application that means diversion. After all, the root simply means "to hold," as also in *attainment, retainment,* or *tenacity.* Entertainment was once supposed to hold people's interest in between (*entre/ inter*) doing other things. It wasn't a model for living.

✦ ✦ ✦

Delight/Instruct/Sell

And what are we to make of the coinage "info-mercial"? On the face of it, the word refers to the presentation of information to advance a commercial or sales interest. However, since advertisements (commercials) have long used entertainment to persuade, the word *commercial* itself has acquired a hybrid connotation of diversion and sales. It's hard not to see some degradation of learning in the idea it must be disguised as escapism, consumerism, or a mindless pastime to be palatable.

✦ ✦ ✦

Teaching

Education is much concerned with teaching, the art of facilitating learning. Teaching is not the only factor that produces learning, but in most cases, it expedites the process. Indeed, in a great many cases, learning would not take place at all in the absence of teaching. Though not all teaching generates learning, poor teaching can impede it.

Teaching is the broadest term for what learning facilitators do. Specific forms of teaching include coaching, explaining, demonstrating, lecturing, training, discussion leading, questioning, critiquing, and so on.

Business, where most officially sanctioned instruction is correctly labeled "training," seldom uses the word *teaching*. Supervising, modeling, coaching, and consulting are other types of teaching that business uses to varying degrees. The business word for the education of an individual is *development*. There is no broad term in business for teaching, despite its occasional advocacy of educational values. (See Training; Development.)

Team

A team is a group of people pursuing a common purpose through combined effort. In schools, the word has been applied most consistently to athletics.

Though draft animals yoked together to perform work are also called teams, the business use of the word derives from the world of school—and professional—sports.

The idea of a team taps into the strongest emotional poles (love brother; hate other) and suggests a fierce dedication to a single cause in a way that none of the other collective-effort words (*committee, ensemble, group, network*, etc.) do. The American glorification of teams may be necessary to balance the destructive selfishness of what we choose to call individualism.

Team Building

Team building refers to a conscious effort to encourage groups of people to work together in the business world as if they were teams. There are probably as many training techniques, interventions, and consultation services available to foster that end as there are factors that block teamwork (e.g., individual ambition, individually based reward systems, internal rivalry and competition, poor communication, prejudice and intolerance, fear of honesty, inconsistent messages from the "top," etc.)

The closest expression in the field of education for allegiance to corporate culture is "school spirit," and it has always depended for its success on the willingness of all individuals to identify personally with the fortunes of official athletic teams. Intellectual achievement itself is for the most part considered a solitary attainment, curiously divorced from everything else in the educational environment. An observer from outer space might be pardoned for thinking that learning takes place in spite of the group, not because of it.

Teamwork, where it does exist or is desired in an academic setting, is called positive interdependence (Arthur Ellis and Jeffrey Fouts, *Research on Educational Innovations*, p. 118).

Team Performance (Evaluation and Reward)

At the core of team performance reviews are very fundamental feelings about justice we all intuit as children: "Why should I be punished for what Mary did or didn't do?" "Why should I share my cake with Johnny when he didn't help?" Most companies are in early stages of experimentation with ways to recognize and reward group performance.

The team approach is also unsettling assumptions about who evaluates whom. Peer review, 360-degree feedback, upward appraisal are some of the names for breaking out of the boss-grading-subordinate evaluation systems. A possible complication is that there is still usually only one source of reward and advancement, a fact that suggests there's only one person to please: the boss.

Many advocates of school reform also want to grade or evaluate group performance. Individual teachers, schools, or systems, they say, should be judged by how well their students perform as a group on a test. Observers oriented toward systems thinking point out, among other things, that resources, parents, and communities also need to be considered part of the team that affects group performance.

151

Team Player

A corporate team player has historically been a person who is willing to go along with the group—or corporate—wishes. Such a person is one who will play ball.

Teachers may label group-oriented behavior in a variety of ways: cooperation, dependence, cooperative learning, peer orientation, conformity, unwillingness to think for him- or herself, inability to work independently.

Business and education generally use the same names for people who don't go along with the group: lone wolf, lone ranger, maverick, nerd, star, prima donna. Whether we approve or disapprove of such people depends on whether or not they appear successful. The truth is that we need joiners as well as loners, but we seem to have trouble recognizing both within the same system.

Team Teaching (and Self-Managed Teams)

It may dismay some in corporate circles to consider team teaching as the educational forerunner of self-managed teams. But such a comparison is possible.

When team teaching was introduced in the 1960s and early 1970s, the idea was to draw on the individual strengths of teachers, to take a unified, interdisciplinary approach to curriculum, and to increase flexibility in a variety of ways. Student-teacher ratios could be varied, individual learning styles and student needs accommodated, scheduling for fieldwork and individual projects more readily arranged, and so on (Robin Barrow and Geoffrey Milburn, *A Critical Dictionary of Educational Concepts*, 2d ed.).

Corporate leaders express these ideals as drawing on individual strengths to enhance group performance, solving problems through a cross-functional approach, and accommodating diversity and flexible scheduling for enhanced productivity.

What went wrong in the early days of team teaching? According to Barrow and Milburn, not all disciplines lent themselves equally well to the approach, there were personality clashes and leadership problems, the schools used it as way to cut back on teachers, and ultimately, test scores didn't improve. In business translation, benchmarking was used without considering local culture, there was a lack of genuine commitment from top management, it was used as a part of downsizing without any real change of culture, and the bottom line said it didn't work.

Tenure

In business, *tenure* refers to the period of time one has worked in a position or at an organization. In education, it refers to the right formally and officially bestowed, usually after adjudication, to remain in a position forever. It amounts to making the social compact binding. The closest business analog would perhaps be seniority in a unionized setting or the lifetime employment policy that distinguished Japanese companies or IBM.

The original rationale for academic tenure was to guarantee freedom of inquiry and expression for those operating in another paradigm. (See Paradigm, Paradigm Shift.) Many question the need for it in contemporary America. Perhaps the best analog would be with professional athletes who receive extraordinary salaries supposedly because they have such short careers. In the case of teachers, one wonders if they were guaranteed long careers to compensate for inadequate salaries. Those who depend on external motivators, and discount such factors as dedication, socialization, professional pride, personal ambition, and love of recognition, believe that in removing fear of dismissal, seniority and tenure undermine performance.

Thinking, Thinking Skills

Thinking may be too humdrum a word to get much notice. Educators seem to feel the need to dress it up (i.e., thinking skills, critical thinking).

Businesspeople seldom mention it at all. Their chief cognitive functions are planning, decision making, and problem solving.

Two points about thinking that deserve notice are these. First, human beings need mental categories to start thinking and then they have to suspend or discard them to *keep* thinking. Mental constructs both enhance and block thinking.

Second, the old-fashioned moral quality of honesty does wonders for a person's ability to think—even when the world doesn't regard that person as very smart.

Time

The time issue in education is "not enough." In business, it's "too much"— that is, those who take too long lose.

Time, Space, and Waste: The Factory Model Revisited

Historically, the business interest in time has centered on speed and efficiency. Information-age technology has liberated time the way machines often do, by being more productive than human hands and brains. It's also compressed time by creating a self-proliferating, international information network: the more information, the more time needed to process and react to it, a cycle generating further information. Unplugging for a while, even to breathe, entails a cost in the global competition. Finally, by democratizing information, the information age is generating a culture that most find more time consuming to manage. Increased access to information necessitates inclusion of more people in decision-making processes. This is not as time efficient as giving orders.

To complicate the time factor more, these technological changes also coincide in America with a major change in the gender and ethnic composition of the workforce. Some of the new working populations have views of time that differ from the white-male, industrial-age model, and the multiplicity of value systems themselves requires additional time for discussion or negotiation.

These are the current time pressures in the business world. In schools, a strong component in the time dilemma is a conflict between managing people as homogeneous groups and as individuals needing different treatment. Perhaps some of the demands of the new information age and the new knowledge workers have first been experienced in our oldest learning organizations. No wonder we've had trouble with the factory model.

In schools, for example, socialization and efficiency would seem to require that students be processed in blocks, kept busy, or at least watched, as much of the time as possible. To keep down labor costs, student services should be standardized, doled out in batches by single teachers. And from the old factory standpoint, the ideal is clear: all real estate should be used at all times by the maximum number of paying units (the students) and serviced by the minimal number of boughten units (teachers).

But schools can never be efficient in that way, nor should they be. The efficiency ideal of the perfect factory, with all classes exactly the same size, would be possible only if the parts were uniform and interchangeable, if fluxes in demand, say, between algebra and geometry didn't occur, and if the clients were given no choice. Besides, not all kinds of learning can be accomplished en masse. As Ted Sizer points out, skills are best developed by coaching, and understanding is best served by discussion. These call for tutorials and small classes. Only knowledge can be imparted to large groups—provided students behave (*Horace's Compromise: The Dilemma of the American High School*, pp. 99-119).

Then there are types of learners. The truth is, everybody has special needs. We have learning disabled-children, second-language children, at-risk children, gifted children, and, especially in suburbia, *my* children. We have children who need prodding, structure, greater independence, remediation, closer supervision, more caring and support, larger challenges. In private schools, we have the privileged few, bred on conspicuous waste. All these require labor-intensive treatment.

And if some of the unique needs are to be met by the classroom teacher, student and teacher need to be free at the same time and have a place to meet, a difficult ideal to achieve when both time and space are booked in blocks.

To the business mentality, the sight of an empty classroom is an affront, an obvious example of wasted real estate, paid for but not used. Yet in schools, time is mysteriously interwoven with space. Many a college president, headmaster, or headmistress whose career has run aground on the shoals of fund-raising for new facilities has done so, not really for territory (space), but for time. To some degree, space buys time. The more space there is, the more activities one can run simultaneously and the more meetings of oddball individuals can happen at oddball times.

Can technology, which created the information-age time crunch in business, assist in education? To some extent, it certainly ought to. It's true that learning labs with technologically assisted individual instruction still haven't lived up to our hopes for them, yet more attractive and wondrous improvements seem to spring forth daily. It's reasonable to expect that each new bell-and-whistle combination could reach a new population group. It's also reasonable to remember the large numbers of kids whose best hope is in an individual human saying, "Hey, where were you?"—whether it's face to face or in an interactive video teleconference with a virtual-reality vice-grip on the shoulder.

TQM

TQM, total quality management, is a business coinage that's the linguistic equivalent of a belt and suspenders. The word *quality*, sufficient unto itself, is inflated into *total quality*. Then the essential control word, *management*, is attached.

The term *TQM* is now also used in the world of education, though educators can easily recognize in the principles of the quality movement many familiar concepts, such as cooperative learning, the use of coaching and nonjudgmental supervision, positive reinforcement, and a faith in intrinsic motivation. (See Ron Brandt, "Are We Committed to Quality?" *Educational Leadership,* Nov. 1992.)

Training

Training is a type of teaching that enables the trainee to perform a task by exposure to such methods as observation, imitation, practice and/or reliance on procedure. Training does not call for a theoretical understanding of the tasks or skills being taught. It is performance oriented.

Animals and very young children are trained. Those who are also educated tap into higher powers of reasoning and intelligence. Training is the most important teaching activity in the business world.

Transcript

If employers regarded the process of education as the first job human beings have, they would consider the information the transcript suggests about a job applicant's course choices and performance important.

By dismissing this information as not relevant to real work or a real résumé, employers not only lose out on a valuable assessment document, but they make a powerful implicit statement about the trivial place of learning in our civilization.

Discussion Questions

1. Look at the entries on Demographics; Marketing; and reconsider the following from Dress Codes: "Told to do as they please, most people are at a loss and quickly look for someone to imitate. Americans prefer to conform by choice." Do you agree or disagree? Why?
2. What linguistic evidence shows that our culture generally views life as a competitive sport or game?
3. What does this basic comparison imply about motivation? Attitudes toward others? How goals or values are established/set? Our measures of success?
4. Where should the emphasis be placed—on group or individual values—in a learning environment? In a work environment? In society?

U is Understated

Underachieve/er (and Overachiever)

An underachiever is one whose performance does not match the expectations of the evaluator. In education, where there is a long-term commitment to individuals whether they reach their potential or not, the word is often used in a tone of moral disapproval. In business, where it is much easier to dispense with such persons, it may merely signal that documentation should begin in case termination is necessary.

Methods for determining the individual's potential vary. Often it is based on the instinct or intuition of the evaluator. It may also be based on aptitude test scores, especially in academe.

The opposite of an *underachiever* is an *overachiever*, a word which, though equally common in education, is never used in business. In business, an employee would not be labeled an overachiever; instead, the evaluator would merely say something like, "Jones really surprised me!" Educators, in contrast, need the term to create the necessary symmetry with underachievers while upholding the credibility of test scores. The notion that test scores are poor predictors of performance is too inconvenient to consider.

Underdog

Americans are known to favor the underdog. This is a major reason employers prefer not to let lawsuits threatened by disgruntled employees go to jury trial. Ordinary citizens tend to identify with solitary individuals fighting the rich and powerful corporate Goliath—unless the underdog is branded a loser instead.

Essentially, an underdog is someone in a weak position who is seen as having some potential for ultimate, long-term triumph. Businesspeople are likely to take a wait-and-see attitude toward underdogs. Teachers often feel protective of them and go out of their way to help; underdogs can provide the most heart-warming successes.

A loser, in contrast, is not only weak, but also lacks potential, effort, or luck. Nearly everyone seeks distance from losers. Often that distance takes the form of persecution in schools and the workplace.

To repeat: who wins the race has a lot to do with the length of the course. (See Faster.)

Understanding

In educational language, *understanding* means a thorough theoretical grasp of a subject or discipline that allows for the extension of learning through application and inference. Understanding of a subject not only survives the test of experience, it's expanded and deepened by it. It represents both a high and deep degree of learning.

In business, as in the rest of society, *understanding* is not necessarily a prestigious term. It is used far less often as a noun—something that one achieves—than as an adjective—the way a person is. An understanding person is one who accepts, and goes along with, things, circumstances, or people one has no hope of changing. Trainees and subordinates in general must attain understanding. Those at the top want knowledge, whatever educational dictionaries may say.

◆ ◆ ◆

The Revenge of George Denton

George Denton was a big, hulking kid with a gait like Frankenstein's monster. You could tell at a glance he was no athlete, despite his size. You

159

could also tell pretty quickly he was no artist-intellectual either, though he ardently wanted to be one. He wore wire-framed, intellectual-type glasses, and his pale bond hair was cut short in a good-boy style, out of fashion at the time I knew him. He had a shy, gentle manner and spoke with a slight stammer. At school, he frequently performed insipid piano pieces of his own composition with embarrassing passion and tried very, very hard to do well. In a harshly competitive setting, he would have been considered average at best.

George Denton did, however, talk his way into my Advanced Placement English class. The English department didn't recommend him for the course, and the guidance people tried to talk him out of it. But in his shy, quiet way he was very insistent, even downright stubborn. The decision (and burden of being the bad guy) was left up to the instructor, but I didn't mind. This was a permissive climate; nobody was really into screening out unqualified students to keep their collective AP exam scores looking good. If it meant so much to him, I figured, why not let him join the class?

Unfortunately, grades also meant a lot to George—grades in the here and now. The problem was that grades in Advanced Placement courses are supposed to reflect college-level standards. The tangible reward for the course—advanced college placement or credit—may not come until the end, after the final examination. Apart from the quality of the experience itself, the reward for the course is deferred; it may never even come at all.

All year long, George and I struggled. I tried as hard as he did. I gave him lots of encouragement. I was always hopeful and conveyed my confidence in him. I was always diplomatic and courteous, and he appreciated it. And to give us both some credit, he did improve under all the coaching. He learned to write good opening paragraphs; he clearly articulated his thesis and developed it with specific illustrations; he improved in his transitions; he dutifully summed it all up in the end. But the bald truth was, he never had anything worthwhile to say. It wasn't a deficiency of effort or mechanics; it was one of perception. He could follow the form, but he had no insight. It's hard to defend marking somebody down merely for lacking talent—and painful to be forced to do it.

For most of the year, George rested firm in his belief there was a code he could learn to crack. To reflect his improvement and reward his effort, I kept nudging up his grades, but inevitably we reached the impasse, that line even I, with my supple standards, really couldn't cross in good conscience. That's when George started to sour.

U U is Understated

I dreaded returning his papers the way doctors sometimes dread the sight of incurable patients. His humble self-effacement faded, and his questions in private conferences took on a more accusatory, subtly belligerent tone. He suggested that others in the class, who got better grades, didn't work as hard on their papers. I didn't doubt it. Neither did I doubt his unwarranted conviction that I was guilty of favoritism. By the end of the year, we were both relieved to end the association. He went on to the college of his choice and to other, I hoped better, things. I went on to other, ultimately better things as well, and didn't mind letting him slip into my unconscious.

Not long ago, though, I realized his determined spirit has stuck with me over all the years, despite my efforts at suppression.

Substance and imagination aside, George really wasn't a bad writer. And by dint of his own efforts and those of other, much better English teachers than I, he certainly had a solid grasp of the basics. Combining these qualities with his longing to be associated with the arts and with his unshakable reliance on rules and systems, I had, in a dark moment, a sudden flash of heart-warming illumination.

George Denton, it suddenly struck me, has become the editor, the one who writes me so conscientiously every few weeks on different letterheads. Yes, it is George who is that busy, hard-working editor, ever so diplomatically informing me that although my concept is interesting and timely, it—unfortunately—doesn't fit into any of his current niches.

Rarely does life offer such perfect symmetry, an ideal fit! And it serves us right—all of us emergent writers, who masquerade for a time as English teachers and mark the George Dentons of the world down for lacking that certain *je ne sais quoi* we cannot teach. My revelation, moreover, has brought me peace. Ever since I identified George Denton as the editor, I find myself more balanced and philosophical about rejection. In fact, I'm almost relieved that he has a chance to get even. Best of all, I don't have to feel so bad about him any more. He's not only alive, he's doing very well—no thanks to me.

Discussion Questions

1. How can you work long-term student/teacher performance appraisal into a strategic plan?
2. When are the results really in?
3. If knowledge is power, what are intuition and insight?

V is for Value

Value-Added

The term *value-added* originated in the world of manufacturing where it refers to the value or worth that is added to raw materials or commodities at each stage of processing or distribution (*Webster's Ninth New Collegiate Dictionary*). It seems more technical and difficult than it is. It's hard only because it sounds like an adjective but really is a noun and because it reverses the normal English order. If the expression were simply "added value," it would be instantly more intelligible.

Application of this awkward, yet businesslike term has proliferated widely, perhaps recklessly. A free book, for example, is offered to new magazine subscribers as "a value-added service to our subscribers." This sounds good and means next to nothing.

Logically, *value-added* can come only from human beings. It doesn't exist in nature. Still, the less direct an employee's relationship to the organization's product or service, the weaker the claim to contributing value-added and the more expendable the person is by cost accounting principles. Once again, human resource people are working very hard to convince a skeptical audience they contribute value-added, that people as well as things count.

In education, those who consider students the product now refer to the value-added as the learning by which schools increase students' worth. Though this has the virtue of acknowledging that learning is valuable, it also draws on the old mechanistic view of students as passive, industrial-age receptacles. Like so much else in the new corporate language, it sounds positive, yet casts doubt on human worth.

Value Judgment

According to Webster, a value judgment is "a judgment assigning a value (as good or bad) to something." In reality, any judgment is based in some sort of value system. Despite its apparent redundancy, the term is probably helpful in distinguishing observable criteria (such as usefulness or effectiveness) from unspoken standards based on personal belief systems.

Both the business and academic worlds use this term to invalidate a judgment. A value judgment is questionable because it is subjective and fails to meet our demand for scientific truth and accuracy. Value judgments are usually dismissed as second-rate judgments. It is hard to teach values or conduct business according to values in a climate that linguistically discredits them.

Running score:	Good	Bad
	Value-added	Value judgment

Values

In our secular and pluralistic society, the word *values* has become the best and most neutral-sounding term devised so far for the ultimate principles that guide behavior. Morals, virtue, and character have, until recently, had outdated sectarian overtones. (*Character* is making a comeback.) Ethics sounds too intellectual to some; too legalistic to others.

Value is a numerical quantity. It is also the monetary worth or price of something. It is the intensity of a color or the length of a musical note. And because works of art are more often described as valuable than expensive, *value* also acknowledges the validity of discernment, knowledge, and taste in determining ultimate worth (*Webster's Ninth New Collegiate Dictionary*).

All in all, it's a good word with something for everybody, though both

163

business and education work hard to contain its use. (See Value Judgment and Values Clarification.)

Running score: Good   Bad
               Value-added   Value judgment
               Values

Values Clarification

Experts agree that values clarification as a process and activity was the creation of educators, a way to shepherd young people through adolescent confusion without preaching to them. (See Robin Barrow and Geoffrey Milburn, *A Critical Dictionary of Educational Concepts,* 2d ed.)

The chief criticism of the process is that in using the nonjudgmental, nonprescriptive techniques associated with psychotherapy for adults, the process indirectly teaches young people that values are merely matters of opinion. Further, the term *clarification* implies that participants already have values when they start the process, surely an unwarranted assumption. The ultimate outcome, critics say, of nonjudgmental group sharing is covert indoctrination away from traditional values. (See William Kilpatrick, *Why Johnny Can't Tell Right from Wrong: Moral Illiteracy and the Case for Character Education.*)

In business, there is nothing that resembles values clarification, except for specially devised groups working on specific projects with internal or external consultants. (See Value Statement.)

REVIEW. Value-added is good; value judgments are bad; values are good; values clarification may be good, but it arises from and leads to value judgments, which are bad.

Value Statement

In business, values are clarified, not by values clarification, but by a value statement. This is like the corporate credo, the list of what the organization believes and the rules by which it intends to achieve its mission. The value statement is prescriptive, overtly designed to get everyone in line.

This is not to suggest that employees are merely told what to do. Usually, in fact, there is a deliberate attempt to foster participation in developing the statement as a way to build motivation and enhance ownership. (See Ownership.) The avowed purpose of the process, however, is

164

to achieve a corporate view, not an assortment of individual ones, as in values clarification.

Virtue

Virtue, like *duty*, *loyalty*, and *obedience*, is a word once used quite freely in education that has now passed entirely out of existence. It probably was never used much in business.

The core concept of virtue is strength: the strength to do what is right, which in turn comes from the strength of right convictions. The closest word we have for this concept in both business and education is *integrity*, which refers to the strength that comes from cohesiveness of convictions.

Vision

Vision is very much a groundbreaking word for business. It boldly affirms the romantic side of the business nature that has been emerging over the past generation after long suppression and self-censorship.

A vision is something that a person sees, but that is not really (i.e., objectively) there. It is a hallucination that only great and powerful people can have because it comes from a higher source. Organizations are to have a vision of where they are going, something that is loftier—though vaguer—than a plan, objective, or goal. Employees are encouraged to share this vision. Visions may be induced by a process called visioning.

To the extent that educational institutions feel pressured to imitate business, they may also seek visions, as well as missions. This would be an ironic development in that the pragmatically inclined have often dismissed academe as visionary.

Vision versus *Image*

Academics trained in the humanities and letters may find it useful to know that business basically reverses the historical connotations of the words *image* and *vision*. While in the arts, an image is always a sensory representation of something concrete, in business, an image is a perception that is often artificially created without necessarily corresponding to anything real or true. On the other hand, a vision in the arts is the sensory perception of something that transcends concrete reality. It may reflect a higher truth or it may be a delusion. ("Was it a vision," Keats asked, "or a waking dream? . . . Do I wake or sleep?") In business, only the cynical would ask the question.

Vision Statement

One could say that in the vision statement, the right brain makes a left turn. To create a vision statement, one edits the clouds and rainbows out of the vision and distills the results into a phrase or sentence that serves as inspirational company slogan—for example, "to be the leader in nose plug production." "Vision statement" and "mission statement" are now often used interchangeably, though originally, the mission statement was an abbreviated version in one or two paragraphs of the strategic plan.

◆ ◆ ◆

Of Worth and Values—
A Farewell Glance at the Factory Model

We've asked if students are the workers, the product, or the consumers in the education industry. We've also noticed as a passing curiosity that the business community regards the American people as synonymous with the workforce (the supply side). We haven't yet noted that it also regards the American people as, in aggregate, the demand side—the consumer, the customer, the market. Are the properties that make a good consumer the same properties that make a good worker?

Theory says yes. Theory says we want informed, educated consumers. It says our employees are merely our internal customers and should be treated as such. It tells us our employees are our greatest asset (unless it says our customers are).

Theory also suggests that schools should produce lifelong learners who both create new demands and contribute new products and services, all as part of a single learning process. Educated producers would be more sophisticated consumers, creating still more demands.

On the other hand, practice sadly suggests that human beings and their qualities really aren't worth much. Common everyday speech endows abstractions like the economy, the bottom line, and the ROI with needs and desires, the powerful living traits of humanity. At the same time, the human element in business is dehumanized as capital, resources, or costs. The humans that serve humans have very questionable value-added.

To judge our operating assumptions from our commercial practices, people merely want easy, immediate gratification. And again judging from our experience, it's not hard to develop these qualities in people to make them ideal consumers—that is, passive, uncritical, easily manipulated, self-indulgent. Contrary to common criticism, Americans are excellent teachers. We've been successfully training consumers for generations here and now around the globe. Our exported culture could even be our most subversive weapon in the global competition. This is because such well-trained consumers don't make the most responsive classroom students. Nor do they have the sort of qualities one would like to see punching in at work.

Jack Benny used to have a routine in his vaudeville act in which his assistant would run on stage with a gun and demand, "Your money or your life." Thanks to his long-established persona as penny-pincher, Benny had only to turn and look at the audience with an expression of consternation to get a great laugh. For him, "Your money or your life" was a tough decision.

Maybe we need to ask that of ourselves. Maybe it would be healthier all around, and ultimately more productive for business and society, if people were encouraged to seek the good and not just the goods, to work and learn for money and for life.

Discussion Questions

1. What aspects of the information age have intensified our need for intellectual wholeness?
2. Where and how do judgment and wisdom fit into learning in the information age, if at all? Should they?
3. What is gained when pursuing clearly defined goals and objectives? What is lost?

W must be Win-Win

Walk the Talk

What educators call modeling or practicing what one preaches business calls "walking one's talk." It's a commonplace acknowledgment that hypocrisy or lack of follow-through may be a part of doing business, especially given the ebbs and flows of advice from consultants and assorted gurus. "You talk the talk. Will you walk the walk?" is a variation on this formula. Like other expressions (e.g., "where the rubber meets the road" or "pick the low-hanging fruit"), it's a kind of corporate baby talk for purposes of bonding.

What Have You Done for Me Lately?

This is another business expression that recognizes the pervasiveness of ingratitude and shortness of memory.

Teachers don't have a comparable expression. Perhaps the concepts of ingratitude and short memory are too familiar as sources of occupational depression.

What's in It for Me? (WIIFM)

The short and familiar version of this business interrogative is WIIFM. Corporate communicators, managers, and supervisors are often advised to appeal to self-interest when training, informing, proposing, persuading.

In the classroom, the WIIFM principle calls for a lot of modification. For most students, the economic advantages of knowledge and skills are too remote to carry much weight and receive little if any reinforcement from the real world. Few teachers would resort to the WIIFM principle as sole motivator. Besides, many teachers actually regard learning as pleasurable and valuable in and of itself. Some even hope to discourage selfishness.

Whole Child

"Whole child" is an educational coinage to remind educators that maturity calls for a balance of physical, emotional, social, and intellectual qualities. The belief is that to emphasize one or some sides at the expense of others does not foster growth. Schools most successful at producing academic achievement have been criticized for failing—and in many instances, crushing irrevocably—the whole child. Many films and novels have portrayed such schools.

Business doesn't have a term for the whole employee. Generally, the best business practice has been to separate the performance from the person and attend only to the former. Nevertheless, exceptions to that practice abound. In the olden days, a person would be praised for being a "company man," implying that the corporate culture extended to all public aspects of the person's life. To this day, executives and their families are often explicitly counseled in how to live out their corporate-defined roles in the community. Meanwhile, people-oriented organizations, like student-centered schools, extend services to more and more aspects of what was once considered private life—for example, alcohol and drug counseling, stress management, smoking cessation, wellness programs, and so forth. (See Work-and-Family Issues.)

Whole Language

In its broadest sense, whole language is an educational expression of the value of an integrated, interconnected approach to teaching, especially at the elementary school level. Reading skills, proponents maintain, should not be taught as something separate from literature or, for that matter, from learning any other type of content. Overall, advocates of whole-language teaching object to fragmentation—reading versus writing, subject A versus subject B, reading letters versus reading words, and so on

(Robin Barrow and Geoffrey Milburn, *A Critical Dictionary of Educational Concepts,* 2d ed.; Arthur Ellis and Jeffrey Fouts, *Research on Educational Innovations,* chap. 4; *Dictionary of Education).*

Business also wants to break out of narrow specialization and the fragmentation of knowledge and skills. The product of cross-functional training, for example, is both less "professional" and more teachable than traditional specialists. This is also usually the case with any product of well-rounded education.

Win-Win

Negotiators and mediators have found that the best and most workable solutions come when a settlement involves mutual gain rather than the creation of a winner and a loser. The expression "win-win" has been spreading in the popular vocabulary as the concept has gained status.

In the competitive business climate, "It's a win-win situation" is usually said in a tone of pride and amazement; it's the icing on the cake, an unexpected, though frankly unnecessary, bonus to winning.

Academic traditions are more varied. Learning is supposed to advance collaboratively; one builds on the work of predecessors and colleagues. And clearly, no one person's learning is diminished by the learning of another. On the other hand, schools that insist on grading on a curve and prizes at all levels that go to the one who learned first tend to undermine awareness that mutual learning can be a win-win situation. At higher levels of learning, this leads to sabotaging others' research, forcing results, and making premature declarations of discovery.

Wisdom

This is another of those words conspicuous by its absence in both business and academe. Wisdom is not derived by study or reasoning; it is a quality of judgment and balance that comes over time through a habit of honest thought and observation.

From ancient to Renaissance times, our Western culture distinguished between *sapientia* (wisdom, knowledge of the highest things) and *scientia* (know-how, knowledge of facts). Increasingly, however, we've placed the emphasis on know-how. It is, after all, the backbone of our economic success, and our nation is alarmed to perceive it inadequately produced.

When people also express alarm about a lack of leadership or vision, they are really trying to say that we lack wisdom as well as know-how.

People feel the need, but don't know the word for what they're missing. The tendency is to look for a person. Probably, more wise people would come to the fore to contribute if intelligence, thoughtfulness, honesty, and commitment were valued when and where they do occur. Both business and academe could do more at little if any cost to build conditions favorable to wisdom.

Women in Business

The interest of women to business is shifting from their place on the demand side, as consumers, to their role in the supply side, as their proportion of the labor supply expands.

This interest takes a variety of forms and springs from the usual array of motives. Economists, psychologists, and sociologists study the impact of two-income families and working parents on our national culture and purse. Many employers now consider workers' personal and family needs an aspect of doing business. (See Work-and-Family Issues.) Equity issues involve legal compliance. Sometimes, they turn philosophical.

Do equality and fairness mean sameness? Do the new corporations value heterogeneity (called diversity) or homogeneity (called esprit de corps, corporate culture, teamwork)? Such questions take on greater intensity when applied to what were once termed opposite sexes. A particularly interesting area of controversy revolves around the question of a female style of management.

Many who believe women managers have a preference for a consensus-building, inclusive, interactive, process-oriented style that seeks win-win solutions point out that this is exactly what management gurus have been advocating to make business more responsive, flexible, and competitive. Those who differ say centuries of powerlessness have left women subservient, indecisive, and too eager to please and that they must learn to empower themselves by studying males and getting rid of self-defeating habits. Still others think gender differences are grossly exaggerated.

Women in Education

Education has a longer history of having integrated women, to some degree, into its operations. Nevertheless, it's also responding to new women-related concerns.

On the process side are questions of gender differences in preferred learning style and of gender bias in teaching and classroom management. Some studies suggest a female preference for discussion, cooperation, collaboration, and interaction with people in the learning process, and a male preference for individuality, autonomy, competition, and interaction with things. Studies of gender bias in teaching have observed that teachers (of both sexes) call on and encourage boys much more frequently than girls and that schools, like the rest of our culture, reward assertive/aggressive behavior. Such practices limit the participation of any who are socialized to more restrained norms.

In the content area, the women's movement has produced the field of women's studies and been part of the challenge to the canon. (See Canon.)

Work-and-Family Issues

Work-family, work/family, and work-and-family issues are the rather clumsy and unsatisfying formulations for the nontraditional view of employees as whole persons.

Given the composition of the new workforce, the thought process goes, it is in the interest of productivity and the bottom line to consider alternative work arrangements (flextime, job sharing, telecommuting), to assist with dependent care arrangements, and to help employees cope with the stresses of life. After all, only a small minority of American families now have one full-time, stay-at-home member who looks after family needs.

Tradition teaches that it's unprofessional to bring personal problems to work. Such a view sees work-and-family assistance as the ultimate coddling to whining workers, a kind of rococo twist to corporate paternalism, coming ironically at the very time when companies are trying to off-load the last vestiges of the old forms—the social compact and guarantees of health care and retirement benefits.

In what seems to be a movement to extend free enterprise social security from cradle to grave, American business begins to sound more like the American school.

Workforce

This is the collective name for all the employees in an industry, plant, or business, for all the workers in a nation, and loosely, for the next generation of people. (See People.) The term *force* comes from the military, and the word *workforce* implies that employees are as homogeneous and unified as a military phalanx. It was coined during the World War II era, probably as a way of encouraging civilians to consider their work part of the war effort and every bit as valuable as combat. In many respects, it could be suspected of being out of tune with future-oriented thinking and even with the realities of our clearly emerging "Workforce 2000."

In keeping with the educational preference for organic over military metaphors, students are called the student body, not the student force.

Workforce 2000

This well-known term comes from the Hudson Institute's study of the same name, which predicted in 1987 that by the year 2000, 85 percent of all new entrants into the American workforce would be women and minorities. Many were shocked to consider an America in which there would, in fact, be no majority. Some white males even confessed to feeling like an endangered species.

Notable features of the Workforce 2000 are increased representation of immigrants lacking English skills, of older workers lacking current skills, and of younger workers lacking basic skills.

Even if Americans had been proud of every feature of their educational system at the time of the study, *Workforce 2000* would have had enormous educational implications. Immigrant workers, older workers, and previously disenfranchised workers all need new, better, and more ways to learn.

Workforce 2000 generated a lot of fear. But it also depicts our era as a most opportune and exciting time for those who yearn for the advancement of learning.

✦ ✦ ✦

To Husband People and Value Learning

The expression that "a woman's place is in the home" is very old, and the objection to it is probably older than we think. It's interesting that there are no expressions about

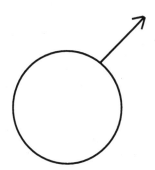

173

where a man's place is. It's not the market- or workplace; it's not the battlefield or hunting ground. Men don't have a place. Theoretically, they're free to choose. It's true that "a man's home is his castle," but he surely is under no obligation to stay there. The symbol itself for male, supposedly a stylized rendering of the shield and spear of Mars, even looks like it wants to go somewhere else.

Historically, nomads (and hunters and warriors) have looked down on tillers of the soil, as men have on women, as line has on staff, and possibly, as commerce and industry have on academe. This tradition has continued even though (or perhaps because) the agricultural phase represents a further step toward civilization. Then again, it's historians and anthropologists (academics) who say so. Though not all possess it, the desire to be on the move is deeply ingrained in the species. All our best stories, going back to Odysseus, Aeneus, and the Patriarchs, are about travelers. It's hard to think of a good story about a man who stayed at home. While originally, the Old English word *wife* meant merely woman, a *husband* was a peasant who owned his own house (*hus*)—literally, a man who dwelled at home. It doesn't sound a very enviable or noble state.

Even something as highly evolved as strategic planning translates into our adventuring spirit. We project into the future and often represent that projection spatially (left to right, bottom to top, ascending slope, taller bars, bigger pie segments). Desired change is represented as conquest, whether or not we choose to hold the new territory or merely exploit its resources. I believe there is a particular love of abstractions among those attuned to this vision of conquest. It is easier to deploy pins on the battle map—troops, forces, capital, and resources—than Mary, José, or Aunt Jessica's mahogany breakfront. These things get in the way. (Note: the Latin for furniture or baggage is *impedimenta*—clearly, a soldier's point of view.)

There are other ways to represent or visualize conquest. "Bionomics," for example, is a new way to look at economics, in which its creator, Michael Rothschild, examines our inherited metaphors critically (*Bionomics: Economy as Ecosystem*). He argues that the information-age economy should no longer be thought of as the industrial-age machine (to be jumpstarted or fine tuned or have its pump primed or its hood looked under), but as an evolving ecosystem that can grow naturally and spontaneously.

The *eco-* metaphor seems more in tune with our emerging sensibility, but metaphors are insidious things, and this one has a metaphor within a metaphor. The ecosystem Rothschild has in mind is a Darwinian rain forest in which innovation and market competition have replaced mutation and natural selection. Companies-species struggle for survival in Darwin's battlefield-jungle. The war metaphor again.

Why not consider still other organic metaphors, perhaps those that are closer to home? Agriculture is a uniquely human activity, a definite design upgrade over fighting a saber-toothed tiger for a downed gazelle. After all, if prehistoric human beings had felt truly at home with "nature red in tooth and claw," they wouldn't have worked so hard to move on to something better.

Farming and gardening call for planning, for controlling, and for fighting adversity, which we humans seem so much to like. They also call for responsiveness, adaptability, and evolution. Farmers and gardeners also always recognize there are elements they cannot control; patience and stoicism have a place, as well as courage, innovation, and perseverance. When individual survival is threatened, the community closes ranks to preserve the species (an animal behavior, incidentally, that some biologists find far more consistent with reality than "nature red in tooth and claw").

As we end a century and an era, we talk of "new fatherhood." We talk of work-and-family, with hyphens. Perhaps in this climate, *husband* will reemerge as a verb: "to husband one's resources," to tend, develop, care for, preserve, protect. Maybe crops can be rotated and diversified. Maybe it's good occasionally to leave a field fallow. Maybe human beings can be cultivated and developed. Maybe life cycles and seasons can be acknowledged. Maybe change can lie in development, evolution, and redefinition as well as in new conquests. Maybe the movement of minds and hearts is also a noble adventure.

Discussion Questions

1. How do gender studies, new-age thinking, and cutting-edge management theory and practice emphasize cooperation and identification with the group?
2. How do these same forces value individual differences?
3. Does the importance of group values (being like others) conflict with the importance of individual values (being unique, different from others) in theory? In practice?

X, Y, Z: Yin, Yang, and NA

Theories X and Y

It was MIT's Douglas McGregor who coined the labels "Theory X" and "Theory Y" to characterize the assumptions behind two prevailing styles of management (*The Human Side of Enterprise*). Theory X assumes that people dislike work and responsibility and will avoid them, that most people lack ambition and must be forced to work, that most prefer being directed and seek security above all else (pp. 33-34).

Theory Y assumes it is as natural to put energy into work as into play, that average people will take responsibility for self-direction when they feel committed to objectives, that imagination, intelligence, and ingenuity are widely distributed in the human race (even though they are underutilized in modern industrial life) (pp. 47-48).

Business, like our other cultural institutions, has been predominantly Theory X in outlook. The cultural changes under way in business for the past decades have been in the direction of X to Y.

Still, most people would understand, with historical correctness, that when schools are told to mean business that means getting serious, getting strict, monitoring, punishing: getting "X-y." The prevailing criticism of schools is that they're too soft and indulgent, perhaps from a large infusion of theory Y thinking in the 1960s. In truth, though, the Y tradition in education is at least as old as François Rabelais.

◆ ◆ ◆

Is Mutual Learning Possible?

Can one institution in transition itself serve as a model for another? Can two very different institutions simultaneously strengthen themselves from within *and* borrow and adapt useful ideas from other institutions? It seems that they ought to.

For purposes of comparison, we could say that the function of business in society is to raise the standard of living and that its opportunities and limitations are based in the global economy. We could say that the function of education in society is to improve the quality of life and that its opportunities and limitations are based in national and international cultures.

Both institutions now need a greater integration of knowledge and ways to encourage thinking and creativity. Each would strengthen itself and complement the other by devising new and better ways to value human beings and learning.

To offset imbalances of the past, business is trying to build cooperation, trust, and shared learning. To offset imbalances of the past, education is trying to build links between classroom expectations and the demands of the workplace.

Both institutions by default have had to fill gaps created by other holes in our society (church, state, family), and this strains what they're designed to do. In some ways, they've increasingly subverted each other, but the answer to that imbalance is not a merger of purpose.

Education always has

a larger purpose than business. It works with the youngest, most fragile, and most impressionable members of our society and sustains some of the wisest, most promising, and talented. One of its functions is to open options and opportunities for living (including alternatives to commerce). We can't base our entire society on the interests and objectives of business, not because they're "bad," but because they're too small to serve our whole society. Strange as it may sound, money isn't everything.

To some extent, tension between these institutions is inevitable. Perhaps the tug and pull where their interests differ is the tacking that will help us sail ahead.

◆ ◆ ◆

Theory Z

Theory Z is the name William Ouchi, alluding to McGregor's work, coined for the Japanese-style management principles that some maverick American companies were using with great success (*Theory Z: How American Business Can Meet the Japanese Challenge*). Theory Z believes that the key to productivity is worker involvement, which is gained in an atmosphere of trust, subtlety, and intimacy. Trust means in part that workers are not demotivated by close supervision; subtlety means the freedom of managers and supervisors to base decisions on their knowledge of workers rather than ironclad bureaucratic rules; intimacy means a "wholistic" [*sic*] valuing of workers as people. Ouchi calls American companies that practice these principles Type Z organizations and companies that are managed along the traditional Western hierarchical or bureaucratic model, Type A organizations (pp. 5-10).

Most good teachers create a Z atmosphere in their classrooms. Perhaps good teachers burn out because it is hard to keep your Z when your organization is an A- -.

Zero Defects

This was one of the earliest expressions of what became the quality movement. Notice that the ideal was cast in the negative form of "no mistakes." It's hard to tell if this was asking too much or too little.

Zero Sum

In zero-sum games, players are completely opposed to one another. What one wins, another loses; thus, the total payoff of the game is always equal to zero. (My $15 win is your $15 loss.) There are other types of games calling for other types of strategies. Unfortunately, our tradition of impoverished choices has created the habit of regarding most human experiences as a zero-sum game (e.g., your happiness must mean my unhappiness).

This is not even the reality for something as seemingly quantifiable as money. It's well known that you have to spend money (like loaves and fishes?) to make it.

Zip

Zip amounts to the same in business and in education: zero. It is also a word for closure. Does this suggest that openness leads to something and closure to nothing? We don't know. But it's the word with which we say farewell.

Discussion Questions

1. What can education and business learn from each other?
2. What sort of relationship should they have?
3. What are the proper limits of that relationship?

Appendixes

A Guide to Educational Poles

A primary purpose of this book has been to highlight the assumptions concealed in common language by looking at individual, everyday words. This appendix suggests that ideas about education also tend to cluster in characteristic patterns and that certain key concepts could imply an entire belief system. As we'll see, the ideas and values that often cluster may have a logical connection—or they may not. The observations that follow, then, are meant to suggest possible patterns a wise listener would seek to explore. Overall, the best policy when discussing education issues is the advice frequently given to new teachers: "Don't take anything for granted."

Preservation and Change

After everyone has agreed that the purpose of education is to pass along the torch of civilization to the next generation and to prepare its members for productive roles in society, it's important to find out who dwells on the idea of sustaining the old flame and who responds to the idea of covering new ground with it. In other words, there can be a crucial difference in emphasis between preserving a commonly understood society, culture, and value system or carrying them on to an envisioned next step. This preservation/change choice is not, certainly, an either/or proposition; it's a question of emphasis or position on a spectrum. Yet from that position many other judgments and preferences often follow.

Another point to note here is that though there may be some overlap, preservation and change are not synonymous with the political positions, conservative and progressive. It is quite common for people to be political progressives, but educational conservatives. The stereotypical college professor, for example, would be a political liberal who values traditional culture, standard usage, and established scholarly methods. By the same token, some of the greatest changes advocated in educational reform (voucher systems, privatization) have come from politically conservative business or church groups. Besides, as elections repeatedly prove, people can vigorously agree they want change, only to find out later they differ on the direction the change should take.

Teacher-Centered and Student-Centered Instruction

It would be logical for people who emphasize the importance of education as a force for preservation to incline toward a teacher- or authority-centered, top-down approach to teaching. After all, the elders of the tribe are the ones who know what knowledge must be carried forward and what skills are essential to the survival of the species. They are also best qualified to judge how and when the knowledge is gained and the skills mastered.

The same teacher-centered approach can also appeal at the change end of the spectrum. There, the authority of the elder would come as the leader with the vision of where the tribe is heading or ought to head. (Opponents might call this social engineering.) On the other hand, to the extent that future needs may be something merely glimpsed or understood only in part, the teacher may be more disposed to play the role of facilitator to what emerges, bottom up, from individual students as unique, active learners. All are part of a dynamic process. In such a case, then, the teaching among those oriented toward change is more inclined to be student-centered to a degree that departs from tradition.

Group and Individual Values

The distinction between group and individual values is always tricky because American culture is extremely contradictory on these values. (More of the complexities are described in the section on "Self and Others," appendix 1.) Officially, we claim to be the land of rugged individualism. We believe that we prevailed over fascism and communism because of our freedom and confidence as individuals. On the other hand, a common criticism of American culture, from both foreign and homegrown observers, has long been that we behave in our mass culture like unthinking herd animals. You could say that true individualism is something our received culture approves, but that most of our existing social institutions do not reward. Theoretically and philosophically, we applaud it; socially and behaviorally, we frown on it.

Then, too, we have had our habitual praise of teamwork more recently reinforced by the elements in gender research, new-age thinking, cultural awareness, and cutting-edge management theory and practice that emphasize the importance of identification with the group. These same recent forces, however, also strongly value individual differences as "diversity" or "multiculturalism." Our received culture stresses competition among individuals and groups; our newer ideas stress cooperation.

184

In education, it would be logical for those who emphasize the mission of cultural preservation to attach more importance to the interests of the group—of society, social role, and common culture. The reason is that this view of education orients students toward an existing culture and shows how they must mold themselves in order to fit into productive roles. The individual is shaped to serve the interests of the group. Both teacher-centered instruction and an emphasis on the interests of the social group over the needs or desires of the individual are especially appropriate in times of stability or in unstable times longing for stability.

Environments that obviously attach value to the individual would logically favor student-centered instruction, where the student, to varying degrees, collaborates on setting the substance, style, and direction of the learning. To the extent that this type of learning is less predictable and less tightly controlled by the teacher, it accords better with a model of education as contributing to social change.

Again, the traditional teaching approach has encouraged competition among individual students, yet often to serve standard, uniform results. Cooperative learning in groups is now widely recognized as an effective instructional approach. Whether it brings out or suppresses unique, individual expression probably remains to be seen.

Sensibles and Intuitives

Many readers are no doubt familiar with the Myers-Briggs Type Indicator, a test that distinguishes sixteen different temperaments on the basis of four polarities Karl Jung originally identified in the 1920s. Of the four polarities, the biggest gap is between so-called sensible and intuitive people.

To quote and paraphrase from David Keirsey and Marilyn Bates in *Please Understand Me: Character and Temperament Types*, sensible people see themselves as practical; intuitives, as innovative. Sensible people want and believe in facts and experience; intuitives are more drawn to the future, the realm of the possible, and a vision of how reality can be better. According to research Keirsey and Bates cite, the great majority of people (75 percent) regard themselves as sensible. The difference between sensibles and intuitives accounts for the greatest misunderstanding among people (pp. 16-19).

It makes sense, almost as a matter of definition, that a higher proportion of change-oriented people, like teachers and entrepreneurs, are intuitives. But again, *most* people are sensible. (See appendix 2, "Ideas and Things.") The dichotomy between sensibles and intuitives, as we'll see, runs throughout many of the choices described below.

Parts and Wholes

Educators have long recognized that some learners proceed from parts to wholes and others from wholes to parts.

In these learning differences, it's tempting to see some correlation with the difference between sensibles and intuitives, and to some extent, though perhaps coincidentally, with one's position on the preservation-change spectrum. The sensible person believes in the ancient Greek adage that "nothing comes from nothing." With their literal, matter-of-fact outlook, sensibles are probably most

185

comfortable learning step by step in observable, measurable units. One masters piece by piece to gain the whole.

On the other hand, the intuitive, according to Keirsey and Bates, "sometimes finds complex ideas coming to him as a complete whole, unable to explain how he knew. These visions, intuitions, or hunches may show up in any realm—technology, sciences, mathematics, philosophy, the arts, or one's social life" (*Please Understand Me*, p. 18).

In the model of education as transmitter and preserver of culture, the institution's knowledge bearers can set clear learning objectives and determine when these objectives are met. For more complex learning, they can establish the parts that lead to the desired whole and the sequence by which the parts are best mastered. Learning can be conveniently organized as a series of finite, predictable, defined experiences in which knowledge is acquired and socially beneficial skills are mastered. Achievement criteria can be measured along the way through testing. In such an environment, having people spring off in pursuit of their own ideas could be disruptive. Generally speaking, analytical methods and departmental organization harmonize with such a world.

A learning institution oriented more toward change is also more likely to see education as an open-ended process, less predictable or finite. It might—but not necessarily—be less disposed toward measurable objectives. As reverence for traditionally received boundaries diminishes, organizations are more receptive to fluid approaches to learning and structure: interdisciplinary area studies, for example, and the whole-language approach. Synthesis and integration are valued; tolerance of difference and ambiguity may also be. Finally, the more student-centered the approach to instruction, the more varieties of evaluation techniques are apt to be used.

Students and education consumers who like expectations and methods clearly spelled out may find such an approach to education unsettling, annoyingly vague, perhaps even threatening. On the other hand, intuitive learners can find teaching approaches that lead step by step to an inexorably predetermined end too regimented, possibly even stultifying.

Each type of learner finds it difficult to flourish in a setting for the opposite style.

Traditional Culture, Pop Culture, Counterculture, No Culture, Cultural Diversity, and Cultural Literacy

One would think that traditional or high culture would be valued more at the preservation end of the spectrum and less valued at the change end; however, this is not necessarily the case. One is well advised to ask for a definition whenever people refer to *culture*. Often, no matter what word they put in front of it, they mean only those aspects of it with which they agree. The word *traditional* is also usually loaded. Again, it often seems to mean nothing beyond "my customary values." In America, in fact, one part of our traditional culture is to discount high culture as impractical.

Preservers and changers can be equally dogmatic. Some degree of tolerant eclecticism can also occur at almost any point along the preserve/change spectrum. When it comes to cultural values, the most useful point to establish may be the degree of inclusiveness and exclusiveness people find constructive. This, however, is an area in which Americans find it very hard to be honest and accurate without being confrontational.

Internal and External Motivation

It is logically consistent for sensible people, who believe more in things than in ideas, also to believe more in external or extrinsic rewards (recognition, pay raises, status, possessions, good grades, T-shirts, coffee mugs, plaques, tax incentives) than in internal or intrinsic rewards (satisfaction, the pursuit of excellence, joy of learning, and the pleasure of social contribution, revenge, or pointless malice). To be sure, no group has a monopoly on ideals (honor, justice, freedom, humanitarianism), but when it comes to assessments of, and expectations about, the wellsprings of human motives, it is probably safe to assume that about 75 percent ask, "What's your angle?" and that only 25 percent wonder what vision is being called into reality.

For the practical majority, ideals are good, added incentives, good PR, and good propaganda, but they support other more tangible rewards. For intuitives, they can be driving forces sufficient in and of themselves.

In a field like education, so concerned with motivating individuals, if not society, to change, the differences in theories of motivation are as critical as the ones over serving materialistic or idealistic ends.

Self and Others

This is another area of paradox. If the majority of Americans believe that self-interest, enlightened or otherwise, drives the world and that self-reliance is a cardinal virtue, why is there so much objection to, and distrust of, educational goals that speak to self-cultivation and self-expression? The underlying philosophical question is whether self-cultivation culminates in beneficent service to the broader community or to mere selfishness or self-absorption.

Contrary to expectation, people attacked as do-gooders or bleeding hearts tend to emphasize individualism and self-awareness in education. They believe an inner journey results in goodness and that character is developed from within. Equally surprising, people attacked for a selfish pursuit of personal interest tend to emphasize a standardized, homogeneous approach to education. They believe an inner journey leads to immorality and that character is instilled from without. The first group thinks community service is a human impulse. The second group thinks it is a moral obligation. Sometimes, they also think it should be a requirement or a punishment, and sometimes they also object to having it required as an infringement of personal liberty.

One looks for consistency in vain on these topics. The same people may want national standards supported and enforced by national testing, privately run schools, less government, fewer regulations, free-market competition, individualism, more police and prisons. In the other camp, the same people may want individualized instruction, student-centered learning, classroom autonomy, independent project-based learning, portfolio assessment, social legislation, and group power in support of individual differences. Yet another interesting hybrid that has emerged decries national and possibly even community standards, is attracted to home schooling, makes free use of self-paced learning technology, all while pursuing a preestablished curriculum coming from a source of their choosing; individual freedom of choice may be highly valued for adults, yet tightly circumscribed for children and adolescents.

Education and Training

A final distinction that can be useful in looking for patterns of ideas and values is one between training and education. Training, which is narrower and more specific in focus, is very well served by a parts-to-whole approach, teaching to objectives, evaluation by testing, and a performance orientation that is supported by external/extrinsic rewards and, quite possibly, a competitive element as well. These methods are successfully used for adults being retrained as part of their work requirements. Activists who are focusing on preparing the workforce through public education, meaning specifically the students who will not attend college, very often favor this set of choices. Ironically, this climate of training also characterizes much of the education of the elite, whose preparatory schools have groomed them for fulfilling their station in life.

Education, the broader process, can also be well served by these same features but may also use a whole-to-parts approach, an orientation toward future learning ability rather than strictly defined future performance, multiple sets of criteria and methods of evaluation, and an expectation of internal/intrinsic rewards. Such a climate is especially effective with talented students, with self-motivated or previously socialized students, and also with bright students who have been alienated from schools in which nobody listens to them. Likewise, students whose self-esteem has been severely damaged do well with an emphasis on individual values, accompanied with group support of their progress.

Conclusion

It's difficult, of course, to present choices without overpolarizing them for clarity or convenience. One's inclinations may not be laid into the cornerstones or official philosophy of an institution. They may vary with circumstances, subject matter, the times, or mood. At any given moment, though, people prefer emphasizing, as has been noted, a mission of social-cultural preservation or change; a teacher-centered or student-centered approach; a view of learning as mastery of content in a closed, sequential system or as a more open-ended, less-defined process; values based on group or individual needs.

To tap personal experience once more, I find, even as I identify the choices, that I've taught with each of the paired attitudes uppermost in mind and that I've gladly learned in each of the paired environments. Overall, I can say that I have one set of preferences for fields of study in which I have a natural aptitude and another for the areas I find difficult or foreign. The most obvious conclusion to draw is that the success of education begins with a knowledge of the individual student. Given that, one then needs to be able to describe it in intelligible, nonaccusatory language.

Commonly Used/ Confused Philosophical Terms

Learned people often use words in what was originally considered their only correct sense. This is especially true of philosophical terms. Whenever you encounter one of these terms, make sure you know what the user means by it. These words are always loaded.

Ideas and Things

For centuries a great dividing line in philosophy has been between mind and matter: What is real? How do you know what is real? Even if you don't know about psychological research and note only how common philosophical terms have changed through the ages in meaning, you'd come to the conclusion that the sensibles, those who believe in things and solid facts, not vague and slippery ideas, are in the majority.

For example, *Platonist, idealist,* and *realist* all originally referred to thinkers who saw ultimate reality as an idea existing in the mind. In common speech now, *platonic* usually means nonphysical and *idealistic* means naive, inexperienced, and impractical. *Realistic* refers to a person who believes in the reality, not of abstract ideas in the mind, but of things, tangible facts, and observations.

Human Nature

Again, considering changes in philosophical terms, the more jaundiced view of human nature seems consistently to prevail. Repeatedly, we seem to prefer fixing on the half of the glass that's empty. For instance . . .

Skeptical originally meant open-minded, able to suspend belief. Now the word is commonly used to mean predisposed to doubt or disbelieve, reluctant to believe anything. In everyday speech, a skeptic is a "doubting Thomas."

A cynic originally was one who believed that human motivation springs from self-interest. The word *cynical* now is used for those who are predisposed to think ill of people and suspect ulterior motives. The words *skeptical* and *cynical* are also frequently confused. People will often say they are cynical about something when all they mean is that they question it. As optimists, businesspeople would passionately deny they are cynics, even though, philosophically speaking, they are, for they believe in the profit motive.

The Epicurean school of philosophy embraced a refined and temperate cultivation of the self, pleasure, and good taste. Now Epicurean is more often used to mean extremely self-indulgent, gluttonous, or sensual. Stoics, whose beliefs contrast with those of Epicureans, believed in service to the state and self-denial. In contemporary speech, only the part about denial of pain survives in the understanding of the term *stoical.*

In some quarters the word *humanism*, which originally expressed an optimistic faith in human potential, has become shorthand for immorality, self-indulgence, and atheism.

Advocacy of tolerance and consideration for individual differences has been labeled "political correctness," a phrase that attributes such an attitude to a desire to appear fashionable. Note how the term ascribes behavior that could come from inner conviction to external motivation. This is cynical in the original sense of the word, for it attributes behavior to self-interest.

Agendas Declared or Undeclared in Education Reform

People often have very different purposes and agendas when they seem to join forces in the same cause. Motives for involvement in school reform can include some of the following:

- *Belief that the economy is hurt by an uncompetitive labor force*
- *Desire to escape or retreat from changes that have already taken place or are under way*
- *Desire for more or different changes in organizational or teaching approaches*
- *Desire to escape from mainstreaming by parents of gifted children or of special-needs children*
- *Tax relief*
- *Corporate interest in wooing next generation (e.g., Apple Computer, Channel 1 advertisers, Disney)*
- *Desire to escape from consumer culture*
- *Union-busting movement in all fields, including education*
- *Desire to shrink government generally, starting with schools*
- *Means of entering the political process (since local school boards may be the most accessible piece of the system)*
- *Generalized response to an individual grievance (e.g., my child's experience)*
- *Disgust with perceived spread of ignorance and incompetence in general population*
- *Religious/moral concerns (e.g., schools should teach character/values more, or schools should meddle with character/values less)*
- *Reports (usually overly simplified, and possibly even inaccurate) on test scores, especially as compared with those of other nations*

Discussion Questions Grouped by Topic

As noted in the preface, discussion questions have been repeated throughout this book to encourage cumulative learning and to emphasize the linking and overlapping of issues. Here they are yet again, this time under topical headings. The letters in parentheses after each question refer to the chapters in which they occur.

Topics

1. *Comparing Businesslike and Academic Outlooks and/or Values*
2. *Motive, Motivation, and Purpose*
3. *Sameness, Difference, and Diversity*
4. *What Should Be Taught and Who Decides*
5. *Fragmentation and Integration, Parts and Wholes*
6. *Evaluation and Measurement*
7. *Relationship Between Business and Academe in Serving Society*

Topic I
Comparing Businesslike and Academic Outlooks and/or Values

How can the differences between Accountability and Responsibility, as described in chapter A, characterize the differences between business and education? (A)
How can the differences between Appraisal and Evaluation do the same? (A)
What evidence is there to suggest that outside of academe, thoughts and ideas are considered unreal and/or unimportant in our culture? (A, B)
Is the bottom line in the financial sense really the bottom line in the common

sense of essence or core meaning? What kinds of people would say that it is and what would be their reasons? What kinds of people would say that it isn't and what would be their reasons? (B)

Does it make sense to use one economic system as a total philosophy of life? (F)

Consider Buy-in; Concern; Interest; Profit Motive. Do we really believe commitment is a matter of self-interest? (O)

What linguistic evidence shows that our culture generally views life as a competitive sport or game? (C, M, T)

What does this basic comparison imply about motivation? Attitudes toward others? How goals or values are established/set? Our measures of success? (C, M, T)

Review Athlete. What is the significance of the athlete for our culture? (C)

List and discuss "E" words suggesting that educational institutions are purveyors of values that are not esteemed in the world of business. (E)

Consider the qualities that make a good person, a good learner, a good worker, and a good businessperson. How are they compatible? How do they conflict? (E, M)

What roles do, or should, effort, respect, and self-esteem play in worker empowerment? (E, F)

What can managers and teachers learn from each other about what to do and what not to do? (E, F)

How do issues of fairness and flexibility fit into the present worlds of business and education? (F)

To what extent does business seem to be adapting attitudes characteristic of education and education of business? (A, F)

How could such a switch be explained? (A, F)

What is gained when pursuing clearly defined goals and objectives? What is lost? (G, K, V)

What is the value of nonjudgmental and nondirective attitudes in an adult psychotherapy group? (N)

What is their value in a business organization that seeks to encourage worker participation, involvement, empowerment? In a culturally diverse business environment? In a high-performance organization or field of endeavor? (N)

What place do nonjudgmental and nondirective attitudes have in an elementary school? In a high school? In a college? In a graduate school? In a department of research and development? (N)

Topic 2
Motive, Motivation, and Purpose

What linguistic evidence shows that our culture generally views life as a competitive sport or game? (C, M, T)

What does this basic comparison imply about motivation? Attitudes toward others? How goals or values are established/set? Our measures of success? (C, M, T)

What obstacles or limitations do schools encounter in motivating performance that business does not? (A, M)

Consider the qualities that make a good person, a good learner, a good worker, and a good businessperson. How are they compatible? How do they conflict? (E, M)

What do your conclusions suggest about teaching and evaluating students? (E, M)

What do they suggest about evaluating teachers? (E, M)

How can parents develop a sense of responsibility in children? How can teachers develop it in students? How can managers and supervisors develop it in employees? (O)

What factors discourage a sense of responsibility? (O)

When is personal involvement in work, studies, or research good? (O)

When is it a problem? (O)

Review Accountability (and Responsibility). What influences our behavior besides rules and laws? (D, R)

What roles do, or should, effort, respect, and self-esteem play in worker empowerment? (E, F)

How do issues of fairness and flexibility fit into the present worlds of business and education? (F)

What can managers and teachers learn from each other about what to do and what not to do? (E, F)

How do you learn best? Working alone for a personally established purpose (e.g., to make my ideal lamp)? Working alone to defeat competition (to make a lamp that's better than Harry's)? Working with others for a mutually established purpose? Working with others to defeat competition? (C)

Which ways of learning do you enjoy most and why? (C)

Locate some people who answer these questions differently and find out how their choices work for them. (C)

Is the bottom line in the financial sense really the bottom line in the common sense of essence or core meaning? What kinds of people would say that it is and what would be their reasons? What kinds of people would say that it isn't and what would be their reasons? (B)

Consider Buy-in; Concern; Interest; Profit Motive. Do we really believe commitment is a matter of self-interest? (O)

Does it make sense to use one economic system as a total philosophy of life? (F)

Topic 3
Sameness, Difference, and Diversity

Does the importance of group values (being like others) conflict with the importance of individual values (being unique, different from others) in theory? In practice? (G, W)

Where should the emphasis be placed—on group or individual values—in a learning environment? In a work environment? In society? (G, T)

How does justice mean treating everyone the same? How does it mean allowing for individual differences? (D, G)

What is gained when pursuing clearly defined goals and objectives? What is lost? (G, K, V)

What is the value of nonjudgmental and nondirective attitudes in an adult psychotherapy group? (N)

What is their value in a business organization that seeks to encourage worker participation, involvement, empowerment? In a culturally diverse business environment? In a high-performance organization or field of endeavor? (N)

What place do nonjudgmental and nondirective attitudes have in an elementary school? In a high school? In a college? In a graduate school? In a department of research and development? (N)

How can we maintain a common cultural heritage if the canon is no longer based on historical significance? (See *"Is* versus *Ought,"* chap. C.)

Do we need a common cultural heritage and language in a global society? (See *"Is* versus *Ought,"* chap. C.)

Why teach the past at all when there is so much new learning to acquire? (See *"Is* versus *Ought,* chap. C.)

Who cares? (And why?) (See *"Is* versus *Ought,"* chap. C.)

How do gender studies, new-age thinking, and cutting-edge management theory and practice emphasize cooperation and identification with the group? (W)

How do these same forces value individual differences? (W)

Look at the entries on Demographics; Marketing; and reconsider the following from Dress Codes: "Told to do as they please, most people are at a loss and quickly look for someone to imitate. Americans prefer to conform by choice." Do you agree or disagree? Why? (T)

Topic 4
What Should Be Taught and Who Decides

Should public education be more centralized (with state or national standards) or more locally controlled (by parents and community standards)? (See Hierarchy in Education, chap. H.)

Are some things more important to learn than others? (See Hierarchy in Education, chap. H.)

Are some people better equipped by virtue of their knowledge, training, judgment, and experience to make these decisions than others? (See Hierarchy in Education, chap. H.)

Are schools in part conveyors of a common cultural heritage or are they only to propagate right thinking as presently or locally understood? (See Hierarchy in Education, chap. H.)

Does taking a vote or survey yield the best result or merely the least divisive one? Must the result be best? (See Hierarchy in Education, chap. H.)

Does education prepare young people for the world as it is or as it should be? (S)

Who decides that question? (S)

Who decides how the world should be? (S)

How can we maintain a common cultural heritage if the canon is no longer based on historical significance? (See *"Is* versus *Ought,"* chap. C.)

Do we need a common cultural heritage and language in a global society? (See *"Is* versus *Ought,"* chap. C.)

Why teach the past at all when there is so much new learning to acquire? (See *"Is* versus *Ought,"* chap. C.)

Who cares? (And why?) (See *"Is* versus *Ought,"* chap. C.)

Topic 5
Fragmentation and Integration, Parts and Wholes

What aspects of the information age have increased our desire for spiritual wholeness? (K)

What aspects have intensified our need for intellectual wholeness? (K; see also discussion questions in chap. V.)

What linguistic evidence is there of a perceived need for wholeness? (S)

How do business and education attempt to integrate information? What else might they do? (K)

What is the difference between knowledge and information? Between knowledge and skills? (K)

Where and how do judgment and wisdom fit into learning in the information age, if at all? Should they? (K, V)

If knowledge is power, what are intuition and insight? (U)

What is gained when pursuing clearly defined goals and objectives? What is lost? (K)

What are the strengths and limitations of experiential learning when it comes to relating parts to wholes? (K)

Ask people how they expand their knowledge and know-how as adults. What background and skills enable them to do that? What do they build on? How do they put the pieces together? How do their answers compare to what works for you? (K)

How do the questions under *"Is* versus *Ought"* (chap. C) and Hierarchy in Education (chap. H) reflect our desire for cultural and social wholeness? (K)

What is [the] value [of nonjudgmental and nondirective attitudes] in a business organization that seeks to encourage worker participation, involvement, empowerment? In a culturally diverse business environment? In a high-performance organization or field of endeavor? (N)

What are the problems with, or limitations of, them in various settings? (N)

What is involved in the ability to create patterns or systems? Recognize them? Work within them? Work around them? (P)

Which abilities are in greatest demand? Which ones does our society reward most? (P)

Topic 6
Evaluation and Measurement

Consider the qualities that make a good person, a good learner, a good worker, and a good businessperson. How are they compatible? How do they conflict? (E, M)

What do your conclusions suggest about teaching and evaluating students? (E, M)

What do they suggest about evaluating teachers? (E, M)

How can you work long-term student/teacher performance appraisal into a strategic plan? When are the results really in? (U)

What is gained when pursuing clearly defined goals and objectives? What is lost? (G, K, V)

What is the difference between "better than all the others" and "the best possible"? Which represents the higher standard? Does competition necessarily determine what is best? (N)

When is it appropriate to measure individual performance against an absolute standard or objective? (N)

When is it appropriate to measure individual performance relative to the performances of other individuals in a group? (N)

Should performance be evaluated solely on the basis of objective factors? Can it be? (O)

Can an evaluator be objective? Should she or he be? (O)

Do you think there is enough coaching and feedback in business? In education? What prevents them? How do coaching and feedback differ from performance appraisal or evaluation? (P)

When does quality represent a minimum standard? When does it represent a high standard? (Q)

In what situations can quality be predetermined and measured? In which ones can it come in unexpected forms? (Q)

Does/should education have any place for variety and the unexpected when encouraging and measuring quality? How about business? (Q)

Review Excellence; Norms. What kind of standards do Americans seem to want? (S)

Topic 7
Relationship Between Business and Academe in Serving Society

Business says it wants leaders. What suggests it really wants followers? How is our educational system geared to produce leaders? How is it geared to produce followers? (P)

What do educators do besides prepare the future workforce in public schools? In private schools? (P)

Do we want members of the next generation to be like each other or unlike each other? (P)

What is involved in the ability to create patterns or systems? Recognize them? Work within them? Work around them? (P)

Which abilities are in greatest demand? Which ones does our society reward most? (P)

What are political skills, how can they be acquired, and how are they used? (P)

Should education prepare people for the world as it is now? How good are we at predicting roles that individuals will play? How good are we at assessing their talents? How good are we at predicting the needs and dynamics of the future? (R)

Does education prepare young people for the world as it is or as it should be? (S)

Who decides that question? (S)

Who decides how the world should be? (S)

What is success? (S)

Do educational institutions convey values that are not esteemed in the world of business? If so, should they continue in this practice? (S)

If knowledge is power, what are intuition and insight? (U)
What can education and business learn from each other? (XYZ)
What sort of relationship should they have? (XYZ)
What are the proper limits of that relationship? (XYZ)

Appendix 4

Alison Kirk is a writer, an editor, and a ghostwriter, chiefly of business publications, who returns regularly to the classroom. As a teacher and an administrator, she has worked at the college and secondary school levels with adult and traditional-age students, rich and poor. Her books and articles on the many facets of human resources have been published nationally, while her personal and humorous essays have appeared frequently in Vermont publications. Kirk received her Ph. D. in English Renaissance literature from the University of Colorado.